Wine

D0970984

by Tara Q. Thomas

A member of Penguin Group (USA) Inc.

ALPHA BOOKS

Published by the Penguin Group

Penguin Group (USA) Inc., 375 Hudson Street, New York, New York 10014, USA

Penguin Group (Canada), 90 Eglinton Avenue East, Suite 700, Toronto, Ontario M4P 2Y3, Canada (a division of Pearson Penguin Canada Inc.)

Penguin Books Ltd., 80 Strand, London WC2R 0RL, England

Penguin Ireland, 25 St. Stephen's Green, Dublin 2, Ireland (a division of Penguin Books Ltd.)

Penguin Group (Australia), 250 Camberwell Road, Camberwell, Victoria 3124, Australia (a division of Pearson Australia Group Pty. Ltd.)

Penguin Books India Pvt. Ltd., 11 Community Centre, Panchsheel Park, New Delhi—110 017, India

Penguin Group (NZ), 67 Apollo Drive, Rosedale, North Shore, Auckland 1311, New Zealand (a division of Pearson New Zealand Ltd.)

Penguin Books (South Africa) (Pty.) Ltd., 24 Sturdee Avenue, Rosebank, Johannesburg 2196, South Africa

Penguin Books Ltd., Registered Offices: 80 Strand, London WC2R 0RL, England

Copyright © 2005 by Tara Q. Thomas

International Standard Book Number: 1-59257-401-7
Library of Congress Catalog Card Number: 2005926964

13   12   11   11   10   9   8

Interpretation of the printing code: The rightmost number of the first series of numbers is the year of the book's printing; the rightmost number of the second series of numbers is the number of the book's printing. For example, a printing code of 05-1 shows that the first printing occurred in 2005.

Printed in the United States of America

Note: This publication contains the opinions and ideas of its author. It is intended to provide helpful and informative material on the subject matter covered. It is sold with the understanding that the author and publisher are not engaged in rendering professional services in the book. If the reader requires personal assistance or advice, a competent professional should be consulted.

The author and publisher specifically disclaim any responsibility for any liability, loss, or risk, personal or otherwise, which is incurred as a consequence, directly or indirectly, of the use and application of any of the contents of this book.

Contents

Part 1: The Basic Basics   1

  1 Get Tasting   3
  2 How to Figure Out What's in
     the Bottle   17
  3 Fearless Restaurant Wine   31

Part 2: Whites: The Big Four   43

  4 Chardonnay   45
  5 Sauvignon Blanc   59
  6 Riesling   67
  7 Pinot Grigio   79

Part 3: Reds: The Big Five   87

  8 Cabernet Sauvignon   89
  9 Merlot   101
 10 Pinot Noir   109
 11 Syrah   119
 12 Zinfandel   129

Part 4: Blends, Bubbles, and Beyond   137

 13 The Best of the Rest   139
 14 All That Sparkles   151
 15 Sweet Endings   161

Appendixes

  A The World's Great Grapes by
     Country   173
  B The Grapes Behind the Names   175
  C Breaking Down the Jargon   177
     Index   189

Introduction

If you've picked up this book, chances are, you think you don't know much about wine. Well, let me tell you this: If you can tell the difference between a lemon and a lime, a pale ale and a stout, or your mom's lasagna and someone else's, you've got the chops to learn about wines. All I'm going to do in this book is give you the basic information that will allow you to feel more confident.

The place most people stumble—I did for years—is when you fall into the idea that wine is somehow far more complicated than food, or beer, or the NYC subway system. It's easy to think that it's terribly confusing, after all, since there are hundreds of different grape varieties, all of which make different wines in different places and can be combined to make even more different types of wines. Add to this the fact that every year's harvest is different, and it's actually impossible to know everything about every wine.

But it's the same deal with food: The possibilities are endless. How do you learn about it? You eat. You watch other people eat. You might read some cookbooks along the way and talk to other people; there's no embarrassment in not knowing just how to go about eating an artichoke, for instance, or how to wield chopsticks.

With wine, you do the same thing: You drink. You taste, you consider. But it doesn't need to end there. We've been raised to think that knowing about wine is the sign of a cultured person, and, therefore, asking about it reveals that you're an idiot. That's a load of hooey. The only people who are idiots when it comes to wine are those who think they know everything.

So this book is meant to fill in for the wine-knowledgeable companions most of us don't have. It'll show you how to open a wine bottle, how to parse the words on the label, how to find your way through a wine list to a delicious bottle. It'll tell you what to expect from some of those most popular types of wines, in both price and flavor, and it'll show you where to look for some lesser-known options that might well cost less and deliver more delicious flavor.

Most important, it'll show you that there's no right and wrong when it comes to wine; there are just different tastes for different people. The goal isn't to become an "expert" for the sake of becoming an expert, but to be able to find more of the wines that make you happy.

So grab a glass and start reading. Cheers!

How to Use This Book

I've set this book up so that you can jump into it wherever you want; if you need rock-bottom basics, like how to get the bottle opened, look to Part One; if it's sparkling wines that pique your interest, flip right to Chapter 14.

I've also set it up so that even when you're short of time or patience, you can flip through the book and check out the sidebars. These boxes hold small bits of important information that will help you learn quickly. I've used four types:

Quick Sip

These sidebars hold important information distilled into its most basic, concise facts, making them easy to digest and remember.

Sour Grapes

Most everything in this book is pretty straight-forward, but a few issues get a little confusing. I've highlighted tricky bits in these sidebars.

Off the Vine

These little boxes hold bonus information: the sort of stuff you don't really need to know about, but you might find interesting or funny.

Winespeak

Although I try to avoid wine jargon as much as possible, some terms come up often, so I've highlighted them here.

Acknowledgments

Thanks to Steven Kolpan at Culinary Institute of America (Hyde Park) for coaxing me into the world of wine, and to Joshua Greene, publisher and editor of *Wine & Spirits Magazine*, for throwing me head-long into it. Thanks also to all the readers of my column in the *Denver Post*, who keep me in touch with reality outside the wine-geek world. And last but not at all least, thanks to Robert Pincus and Dill, for sharing the beers and the excellent times that keep this wine writer going.

Special Thanks to the Technical Reviewer

The Pocket Idiot's Guide to Wine was reviewed by an expert who double-checked the accuracy of what you'll learn here, to help us ensure that this book gives you everything you need to know about wine. Special thanks are extended to John James.

Trademarks

Part 1

The Basic Basics

If you're a little apprehensive about learning about wine, relax right now. It's not that hard. In this part of the book, we'll walk through everything from getting the cork out of the bottle to what to do when you're in a restaurant and someone has done it for you.

Chapter 1

Get Tasting

In This Chapter

- Opening the bottle
- What you need to taste wine
- How to taste
- How to remember what you tasted

News flash! For all the books and classes out there about wine, there's only one way to learn about it: by tasting. You can't learn what wines taste like by reading about them any better than you can discover the taste of whale fat without trying it. And unlike tasting whale fat, tasting wine is fun.

So get a bottle of wine. Right now. It doesn't matter what it is or how much you paid for it. Just pull a bottle off the shelf that looks good to you, take it home, pour yourself a glass, and start reading.

Oh, right: first you have to get the wine out of the bottle. If you're not a whiz with a corkscrew, buy a screw-capped wine (they aren't just for brownbaggers anymore). Or learn. It's not hard.

Opening the Bottle

This is the place a lot of people freak out. Cork-screws do look a little like instruments of medieval torture, but they should torture only the cork, not the user. If you've had one that's never worked well for you, get another one. There's a corkscrew for everyone.

Quick Sip

In the last few years, screwcaps have become a popular alternative to cork—even on wines that cost $100 or more. Not only are screwcapped wines easier to open, but many tests have shown they keep wines fresher tasting for longer times. Screwcaps also reduce the incidence of corked wine, wine that's been infected with bacteria that makes it taste like wet cardboard.

I'll tell you how to use the most popular corkscrew styles in the following sections, but whichever style you opt for, you first must take the capsule off the bottle—that's the plastic, metal, or wax covering over the cork. Waiter's friends come equipped with a small knife that aids in taking it off. Otherwise, buy a capsule cutter: They aren't expensive, and they are much safer than attempting to use the end of the screw. When you get the capsule off, you're ready for the details.

Straight Corkscrew

This is the type of corkscrew that comes folded in your Swiss Army knife. A "worm," is that twisty thing you screw into the cork which is attached to a handle. You just screw the worm in and pull.

- **Pros:** Convenient, affordable
- **Cons:** Removing the cork usually requires holding the bottle between your legs and pulling hard—not a sexy look.

Quick Sip

When using a manual corkscrew, twist the worm in only until you can still see 1.5 to 2 twists. If you go farther, you might go all the way through the cork, pushing bits of it into the wine.

Waiter's Friend

This is the one you see waiters using. Pull the knife out and use it to take the capsule off the bottle. Fold it back in and fold out the worm. Place the tip of the worm just off-center in the cork, and twist it while pushing down slightly until only 1.5 to 2 twists are visible. Position the metal lever against the lip of the bottle. Pull up the handle. If the cork begins to bend or crack, stop and screw the worm in a little more. Then pull out. It might take a couple tries to get the hang of using a waiter's friend, but if every waiter this side of Mars uses it, then they can't all be wrong.

- **Pros:** Convenient, affordable; comes with capsule cutter
- **Cons:** Takes some practice

Winged Double-Lever Pulls

The one your parents had that looks sort of like an angel with wings that go up and down. You screw the worm into the cork and then push down on the wings to remove the cork.

- **Pros:** Easy to set up
- **Cons:** Looks clumsy; requires two hands; doesn't come with a knife to get the capsule off

Ah-So

This is a handle with two parallel strips of metal, one longer than the other. The idea is to slowly, gently wiggle the metal strips between the cork and the bottle, and then slowly, while twisting it, pull out the cork.

- **Pros:** Small, convenient, and fabulous for extracting crumbly or broken corks, and it doesn't puncture the cork—a bonus for cork savers
- **Cons:** Tricky to get the hang of

Lever Pulls

These fit over the neck of the bottle and allow you to pull out the cork with one swift, nearly effortless push and pull of a lever.

- **Pros:** Idiot-proof, great for people with arthritis
- **Cons:** Much larger and more expensive than most other corkscrews; worm needs replacing every 60 to 80 bottles or so.

Bar-Mounted Models

The Cadillac of wine openers, these cork pulls mount on a counter. All you need to do is put the bottle in the contraption and pull the lever up and down.

- **Pros:** Stability, speed, ease
- **Cons:** Expensive, immobile, needs assembly

There are other types of corkscrews out there, many just as good as these. It makes absolutely no difference which type you use. What matters is that you get the bottle open. Grace comes with practice.

Now get a glass. If you don't have any wine glasses yet, don't worry. Use what you have. You may soon find yourself wanting to invest in a set of wine glasses, though. They are designed to give you the most out of every sip.

Quick Sip

What if you get pieces of cork in the wine? No big deal. Just pour the wine through a strainer; the cork won't affect the taste of the wine.

Glassware: Truths and Myths

Choosing wine glasses can be as intimidating as choosing a wine. They come in so many sizes, shapes, and price ranges, and with so much hype, you could drive yourself nuts picking out the perfect ones.

Sour Grapes

You'll often hear people say that red wines need a bigger glass than white wines. Don't believe them. That idea is based on the theory that white wines aren't as interesting as red wines. That may have been true a hundred years ago, but today white wines deserve just as big a glass as reds.

Find a glass that feels good and fits your budget, and buy several. Since glass shape and size can change how a wine is perceived, when you're tasting more than one wine, you'll want to taste it out of the same sort of glass. Likewise, when many people are tasting the same wine, it's better to use the same glasses, or the differences people perceive may be more due to the glass than the wine itself.

What about glasses designed specifically for particular types of wines? Try them, if you want, but don't feel bad if you'd rather spend money on wine than glassware. Expensive glasses won't make a cheap wine taste any better, while great wine will taste good even out of chipped tumblers.

Time to Taste

It sounds strange, but there really is a bit of technique to getting the most out of your glass of wine. The reason so many people get so excited about wine is that it offers lots of different flavors and sensations. It's not the short-lived jolt of refreshment of a cup of lemonade. The flavor of great wine can last for minutes and run through a rainbow of flavors. To enjoy it, it takes time and attention.

Start by pouring just an ounce or two in your wine glass; in a 6-ounce glass, that's not even one third full. (Remember that, for now, you're tasting; you can drink later.)

Then you're going to go over the five S's: see, swirl, smell, sip, and spit or swallow.

We'll go over the whys of each step in detail.

Off the Vine _____

If you want to pour like a pro, hold the bottle so that the label faces the person for whom you're pouring. As you finish pouring, give the bottle a quick, small turn as you snap it up so that it won't drip. Don't hesitate: Wine bottles can smell fear and will drip wine all over if you don't handle them with confidence.

See

Look at the wine. Hold the glass at an angle against something white, to look at the color. This isn't so that you'll look like a snob. You want to know …

- Does it have anything unpleasant-looking in it? In white wines, sometimes you'll see tiny, clear crystals at the bottom of the glass. They are harmless tartaric acid crystals, nothing to worry about. Reds will sometimes have some sediment that settles at the bottom of the glass; this, too, is harmless. What you're looking to avoid is seriously strange stuff. I once poured a glass of wine with a dead bee in it; it must have flown into the bottle just before it was corked.

- Does it look like it should? If you ordered a still red wine but this one is bubbling, then you know something isn't quite right.

- Is it pretty? Enjoying wine involves all the senses: Go ahead and take in the view.

Swirl

Swirl the wine. With the bottom of the glass on the table, move it in small circles so that the wine begins to swirl up the side of the glass. Why? For the same reason you stir a pot of soup when you want to smell it—to get more aroma out of it.

Sniff

Sniff the wine. Go on, get your nose right in there, and take a big sniff. Or take a series of short sniffs—whatever works for you. While you smell it, ask yourself these questions:

- Does it smell good? If the wine has turned to vinegar or is *corked* (that is, infected with a bacterium that makes it smell like wet cardboard), you'll be able to find out now, before you put it in your mouth.

- What does it smell like? It might seem like we're skating into geek territory here, but in fact, most of what we think of as taste is actually smell. Think of how little you can taste when you have a bad cold, or try tasting a wine with your nose plugged. It's nearly impossible to taste anything. So if you don't smell the wine, you'll miss most of the nuances that make it such a delicious, special beverage. And if you don't force yourself to come up with ways of describing it, you'll never remember one wine from the next.

Sour Grapes

Every once in a while, you'll uncork a wine that will smell more like wet cardboard or a musty attic than wine. That wine is **corked**—that is, infected with a bacterium that's harmless to humans but ruins our wines. If this happens to you in a restaurant, immediately tell your waiter; he or she should give you a new bottle. If it happens at home, put the cork back in the bottle and return the corked wine to the store from which you purchased it. The retailer will replace it with another bottle.

Sip

Sip the wine. There's a lot going on in a glass of wine, so take it slowly—a sip, not a gulp, at a time. And instead of immediately swallowing, hold the wine in your mouth and roll it around for a few seconds. If you can, open your mouth a tiny bit and suck air in so that you make a quiet gurgling noise. It sounds weird, but the idea is the same as swirling the wine: By getting more air into the wine, it'll release more aroma, which is the key to maximum flavor enjoyment.

While you're doing this, think about how the wine tastes. Is it sweet or savory? What sort of fruit does it taste like? What else do the flavors bring to mind? Spices? Earth? Bacon? Nail polish remover?

After you swallow, pay attention to the flavor that lingers there—the finish, in wine geek-speak. How long does it last? Does the flavor change as it fades?

Spit or Swallow

If you're tasting lots of wines and you want to remember what you tasted, spit. Professional wine tastings always have buckets around for this purpose, and professionals use them; if you're tasting at home, have some sort of receptacle handy for you and your guests to spit into.

If you're at the dinner table or are tasting just a couple wines for pleasure, go ahead and swallow.

Either way, there's one more thing left to do. If you want to remember which wines you liked and which bottles you hated, you're going to have to write down your impressions.

Taking Notes

Tasting wine is one thing; remembering what different wines taste like is another. So here's where the work begins. You need to take notes.

That's right. Write down the name of the wine, the vintage, and any other identifying information—some people find it helpful to jot down a note on what the label looks like. You can even take the label off to save it (soak the bottle in warm water, or use the special adhesive found in many wine stores designed for label saving), and write your notes next to it.

People often make fun of wine writers for using fanciful descriptions to describe the wines they've tasted, but after you write 20 notes, you'll see why. Describing wines is tricky. "Tastes like red wine" doesn't tell you any more than if you'd said about Dr. Pepper "tastes like soda." The question is, what sort of red wine does it taste like? For this, we need to use similes.

Tastes Like

If you've been tasting wines for 50 years and paying lots of attention, you may well be able to say, "This tastes like Merlot," just as most of us could say of a dish, "This tastes like chicken." But try to describe the flavor of chicken to someone who's never tasted the bird. You'll probably describe the blandness of flavor and the texture, and you might well try to come up with some food that it tastes like—it's bland/delicate like white fish but more meaty, or it tastes like turkey but less gamey.

It's the same thing with wine. Most of us don't know Merlot well enough to say, "Gee, this red wine tastes like Merlot," so the best we can do is try to come up with other, more familiar flavors that will help describe what we're tasting. Merlot, for instance, might remind you of cherries or plums.

Be Imaginative

"Tastes like cherries" helps only if you haven't written it for six other reds—and you probably will have, as cherry is a familiar flavor to most Americans and we use familiar flavors to help us describe flavors in wine. You've got to push yourself further and find more flavors, textures, weights. To form the most complete picture of a wine, you want to describe its ...

- **Color**—Is it ruby or burgundy? Gold or yellow with green tinges?

- **Scent**—What's it remind you of? Fruits? Spices? Earth? Dirty socks? Your dead aunt's perfume? The more personal the recollection, the more memorable the wine—though you might have difficulty explaining yourself to your friends.

- **Flavor**—Same deal as scent, except that here you also want to take into account the following two points:

  - **Texture**—Does the wine feel smooth or gritty? Juicy or drying?

  - **Length**—Does the flavor last a long time, or is it gone in a flash?

Do this for five wines of the same color and look at your notes when you're done. Even on paper, you can tell they are different wines, right?

Oh, there's one more thing to ask yourself—do you like it? If not, cross it off the list. It doesn't matter that your husband or a wine magazine or the guy at the wine store told you it's great. The greatness of wine is subjective. What matters is what *you* think.

 **Sour Grapes**

Describing wine is hard, but don't get intimidated by people who rattle off two dozen fruits and spices they've found in a glass, or those who wax on about the precocity of a little flippant wine with nice legs and a firm kick. No one else will know what he or she is talking about, either.

So now that you know how to taste like a pro, it's time to go shopping. If you keep tasting notes on what you're drinking as you go along, you'll have a list of favorite wines by Chapter 3. Pretty easy, huh?

Chapter 2

How to Figure Out What's in the Bottle

In This Chapter

- What's important on the label
- What to do when there's no grape on the label
- New world vs. old world
- Back-label secrets

Even pros can get cross-eyed looking at all the different wine labels on a wine store's shelves. How do you choose? What should you look for? What does all of the stuff on the wine label mean? Read on and I'll break it down.

Label Basics

Because the front label is the calling card of a wine, winemakers go to great lengths to make their labels stand out on the shelf. Regardless of gold type, fancy designs, or other eye-catching elements, the most important information a wine label offers is …

- Where it's from.
- Who made it.

In addition to these facts, you might find a year, the name of the grape variety from which it's made and a vineyard, a designation of quality, the name of the winemaker's dog, or any number of other words and symbols. These things may or may not tell you much about the wine inside, so let's first stick to the basics.

Where's It From?

Every country, even every winemaking region, has its own style of wines. Knowing even a little bit about a country can help you figure out what sort of wine is inside the bottle. Many places also use appellations, or legally defined place names, which can tell you almost everything you need to know about the wine. The most obvious factor, however, is climate.

Climate

In general, the warmer the climate, the riper the grapes get. And the riper the grapes are, the richer the wine they'll make. That means the same grape can make a light, crisp wine in a cool place, and a richer, fuller-flavored wine in a warmer place.

To remember this, think about fruit in general. Cool regions tend to excel at crisp, crunchy apples, tart gooseberries, tangy currants, and other fruits with lots of acidity. Tropical regions are more famed for sugar-sweet pineapples and mangoes. That's because heat and sun are sugar machines. The more warmth there is, the faster a fruit produces sugar and the faster it looses acidity.

So when you pick up a bottle of wine, think about the climate of the place it comes from, and you'll already have an idea of whether it'll be crisp, tart, bright, and zingy, or lush, round, smooth, and cushy.

Old World vs. New World

In general, the wine world can be broken into the old world and the new world:

- The new world is defined as any country that hasn't been making wine in a big way for centuries. New-world countries include the United States, Canada, South America, Australia, New Zealand, and South Africa.

- Old-world countries have been making wine for centuries, like most of Europe and the Middle East.

It's always dangerous to make generalizations, but in general, if someone says a wine is new world in style, he or she means that it tastes clean and very fruity, and probably has a vanilla sheen from time spent in oak barrels before bottling.

Old-world wines, on the other hand, often have more savory flavors, more earth and mineral flavors than bright fruit or sweet oak. Some can be downright funky, in the delicious, soulful James Brown sense of the word. These hard-to-describe flavors are often referred to as "terroir," meaning, loosely, that they have a flavor that's particular to a specific place.

If you prefer wines with a little good funk, you'll want to spend most of your time looking at wines from the old world. If you're looking for a fruity, flashy wine, then look to the new world.

Appellation

An appellation is the most exacting indication of climate on a bottle of wine. An appellation is a legally defined area that's been singled out because it produces grapes with a certain character reflective of that place—a terroir (tare-*whar*) character. For instance, the Pinot Noir that grows in Sancerre, France, tastes very different from the Pinot Noir grown in Burgundy, France.

The differences between appellations can be determined by temperature, soil, wind, hours of sun, rain, altitude—in essence, any natural factors that affect the flavor of the grapes grown within the boundary and that differentiate them from wines grown outside the boundary. So that vintners outside appellation boundaries don't try to use appellation names for marketing purposes, most countries have systems for regulating appellations. The big ones are as follows:

- France: Appellation d'Origine Controlée (A.O.C.)

- Germany: Qualitätswein bestimmter Anbaugebeite (QbA)
- Italy: Denominazione della Origine Controllata (D.O.C.)
- Spain: Denominacion de Origen (D.O.)
- The United States: American Viticultural Area (A.V.A.)

When you see the name of a place followed by any one of the preceding terms, you can be assured that the wine comes from within the listed region.

Sour Grapes

An appellation isn't necessarily a promise of quality. Some vintners are simply more talented, knowledgeable, or well equipped than their neighbors in the same appellation.

Many appellations contain subappellations, smaller areas that produce wines with even more specific characters. In addition to, or instead of, a general appellation, a wine label might specify the following:

- A district or county
- A village
- A vineyard

These designations tell you that the named area produces wines that stand out from those in the surrounding areas for one reason or another. The grapes may or may not be better; they might just make wines that taste different.

To taste this difference for yourself, find a winery that makes a wine labeled with a general appellation, as well as some vineyard-designated wines within that same appellation. Buy one of each, making sure they are all made from the same grape (the vineyard-designated wines will cost more, since the production will be more limited) and taste them side-by-side. Some of the differences you taste might be the result of winemaking techniques, but the largest difference will be in terroir, or the taste particular to the places the grapes were grown.

This concentration of place doesn't mean that grape varieties don't matter; in fact, many old-world appellations also specify the allowed grape varieties, growing methods, and winemaking techniques. That way, the thinking goes, the buyer is assured of getting the wine one would expect from that region, and the region's wines will retain a clear identity. Chianti, for example, will always taste like Chianti, not California Zinfandel.

Grape Variety

Even if a wine doesn't list a grape on the label, the grape variety is the biggest determinant of the flavor of the wine. Knowing what grape or grapes went into the wine can tell you …

- What color the wine is (sometimes, at any rate).
- The general flavor of the wine.

Of course, you can figure out those things only if you know something about the grape. We'll go over each of the major grape varieties in the chapters that follow and talk about what sorts of wines you can expect from them.

Sour Grapes

Maybe because it makes wine sound fancier than it is, people often refer to grape varieties as varietals. *Varietal*, however, is an adverb; you can have a varietal wine (a wine made from one grape variety), but Syrah is a grape variety, not a varietal.

But don't worry that knowledge of wine grapes is the only way into the wine world. In many wine-growing parts of the world, local wine lovers have no clue what grapes go into the wines their neighbors make. They just know how they taste. As you've read here, you can learn a lot just by knowing what color it is and thinking about where it was grown.

The Smaller Print

Where a wine is from and what grape variety it's made from are the two most important pieces of information offered on a wine bottle, but there are other clues that can give you a clearer picture of what's inside the bottle. You might want to look for …

- Who made it.
- What year it was made in.

- A designation of quality, style, and/or ripeness.

The Name Game

The name of the winemaker isn't always the most helpful info on the wine label, but it's usually the most obvious. Why should you care who made the wine? For the same reason you might care who made your food:

- **Trust**—If the maker makes it difficult to tell who made the wine, then what is it saying about the product inside?

- **Ease**—Just as you have a favorite bread baker, cookie maker, or cereal, as you taste different wines, you'll find that you have favorite wine producers, too. The easiest way to find a wine again is to look for it or ask for it by name. Even if the winery makes several different wines, by remembering the winery, you've narrowed the possibilities to a handful—and chances are, you'll like the rest of the winery's wines, too. That's better than if you remembered that you liked a certain Chardonnay but couldn't remember the name of the maker. That would leave you with slightly less than, oh, maybe 10,000 choices.

Vintage: Mother Nature's Signature

Vintage is the year in which the grapes for the wine were picked, and this date is usually on the front label. If there is no year on the label, you can assume it's a nonvintage wine, which is a round-about way of saying the wine is made of grapes from more than one year.

Why care about the year the grapes were picked? Two reasons. The vintage date can tell you …

- The age of the wine.
- The character of the wine.

As wines get older, they change. White wines tend to get darker, and the bright, fruity flavors they had when they were young become more subdued, soft, nutty, and caramel-like. Red wines become lighter in color and exchange the vibrant fruit of youth for dried fruit flavors, spice, and earthier notes. If you prefer your wines bright and fruity, look for wines that were made within the last few years.

The difference vintage makes in character can be subtler, but think of it this way: You know how some years the strawberries (or whatever fruit grows where you live) in your area are terrific, and other years, they are only so-so? It's the same with wine grapes. If the summer is cooler than usual, the grapes might not get as ripe as they normally do, and the wines that year will have more acidity and thinner flavors than usual. In hot years, the wines might taste more jammy and thick—as if the sun had literally baked the grapes.

 **Sour Grapes**

Though vintage charts are a favorite give-away at wine stores and an addition to wine books, take them lightly. Weather can affect one part of a region more than another, or affect only some grape varieties and not others. So when you see a three-star rating, for instance, you can't know whether it's because one part of the region was decimated by hail, earning one star, while the other half thrived, earning five, or if the whites didn't come out so well but the red wines are excellent. Besides, vintners today have so much knowledge and technology that they can produce excellent wines even in the toughest years.

Generally, you probably won't notice vintage differences unless you taste different vintages of the exact same wine side by side. The only time you'll really want to be concerned about vintage is if you decide to take up cellaring wines from Bordeaux, Barolo, and other places prone to bad weather. Wines from difficult years often won't age as long as wines from better years, so then it pays to pay attention to vintage.

Qualifying Qualifications

Many wine labels boast impressive-sounding terms like Reserve, Special Selection, or Old Vines.

These terms may indicate something special about the wine—or they might just be there to make it sound fancier than it actually is. Here's what you need to know.

Possibly Empty Promises

If a wine label promises a wine that's from "Old Vines" or "Ancient Vines," or is a "Special Reserve," "Vintners Reserve," "Special Cuvee," "Estate," or "Select," in any language, you'll have to take it on good faith. None of these terms has any legal meaning.

Legal Classifications

Some winemaking regions have set up official methods and terms to classify wines by quality. Here are the important ones to know in each country:

France: In Bordeaux, wines are classified in ascending order of quality as Bordeaux, Bordeaux Supérieur, Bordeaux *Cru* Bourgeois, Grand Cru Classé, and Premier Cru. Alsace also calls wines from certain top vineyards Grand Cru. (Confusingly, in Burgundy, Grand Cru wines are ranked more highly than Premier Cru wines.)

Winespeak _____

Cru means vineyard.

Italy: Classico denotes a more specific wine region; for example, Chianti Classico is an area inside of Chianti, the region. Superiore and Riserva are terms used to indicate a wine that's met more stringent quality and age requirements than the basic versions.

Spain: Crianza, Reserva, and Gran Reserva indicate, in that order, increasing levels of quality and age.

Special Techniques

Some wine labels indicate whether the wine inside was made with a special technique, such as …

- **Amarone**—This is an Italian technique using semidried grapes.
- **Ripasso**—Italian for "repassed," ripasso means that the wine has been reunited with its grape must (the pulp left over from pressing) for a spell to take on more flavor from it.
- **Icewine/Eiswein**—This is wine made from frozen grapes.

In Germany, many wines are classified by the ripeness of the grapes at harvest, too, but we'll get to that in Chapter 6, on Rieslings.

There's just one more element of the wine label you want to look at, and it's one that most people ignore: the back label.

The Secret of the Back Label

The back label on a wine bottle—the dull-looking one with the warnings, bar code, and other stuff— holds one of the most powerful pieces of information about any imported wine: the importer.

Knowing who the importer is can help you find the wine again and give you an idea of whether you'll like it.

Tracing Bottles

Say you were given a bottle of wine that you love, but you can't find it in any stores. Just check the back label for the importer, and call the company. The importer can tell you if and where the wine is available in your area.

Importer Style

Many importers specialize in a particular area, like Italy. But for an importer to differentiate his wines from the next guy's, who's also specializing in Italy, he's got to have an angle. It may be that he prefers bigger, richer wines with clean, modern lines, or it might be that he's a strict traditionalist. When you find a wine you like, try to find more wines brought in by that company. You may have found a company with tastes that parallel yours.

About Those Sulfites

The way wine labels in the United States trumpet "Contains sulfites" sure makes it look like they are dangerous things. The truth is that there's little to worry about for the majority of the population.

Sulfites are preservatives that occur naturally in all sorts of fermented foods, including wine, and they are regularly added to packaged foods to retain freshness.

All but a handful of winemakers use sulphur dioxide during winemaking to protect the grapes from oxidizing (reacting with air) and to kill bad bacteria. Wines made without additions of sulphur tend to spoil very easily.

Though the amounts used are typically very small and, in fact, almost always far smaller than would instigate a reaction in the few asthmatics sensitive to sulfites, the U.S. government requires all wines that contain more than 10 ppm of sulfites to state "Contains sulfites" on the label.

So contrary to popular opinion, sulfites do not give wine drinkers headaches. Histamines and phenolics are the likely culprits—but, as there are no warning labels for these components, it's hard to avoid them.

Fearless Restaurant Wine

In This Chapter

- How to love, not fear, the sommelier
- The tasting ritual demystified
- Finding the best deals
- Why wines cost more in restaurants

Now that you've read the first two chapters, you know how to open a bottle of wine like a pro and you can parse every word (well, as many as needed, at any rate) on the label. That means you'll have no problem when you walk into a wine store. But what happens when you're in a restaurant and the waitress hands you a hundred-page wine list? Do you simply ask for a glass of Chardonnay and call it quits?

No! You can combine your knowledge of labels, places, and varieties with some information about how wine lists work to seek out the good bargains. Better yet, you can start believing that the *sommelier* is your friend.

Love the Sommelier

If there's one thing you remember from this entire chapter, make it this: the sommelier is your friend. I don't care how "expert" you are: if you're not asking the restaurant staff for help in choosing wines, you're missing out.

Winespeak

A **sommelier** (some-el-yay) is the person who designs the wine list and helps people find their way through it to a wine they'll love.

Why? Because no one knows the wine list or the food menu as intimately as the people who work in the restaurant, and their insights can steer people to the best wine-and-food fit.

The Sommelier's Job

A sommelier is the person whose job it is to design the wine list and help people find their way through it. Many people still hold an image of a sommelier as an intimidating gatekeeper to the wine list, typically tuxedoed, older, and wearing a silver cup on a chain around his neck like a badge. We worry, "Will he snicker if we order the wrong wine? Will he hit me with that thing?"

Truth is, these days, the sommelier is as likely to be a woman as a man, as young as the rest of the wait-staff, and able to converse as easily about wine as about movies and rock bands. He's in the business because he was bitten by the wine bug and can't afford his hobby otherwise, and he's so keen on it he wants to share it with others. He also knows the menu better than any wine expert. It's his job to help the customers find their way through the wine list, and he can't wait until you call him over.

Your Job

The greatest sommelier in the world will be completely useless to you unless you call on him to help, so your first job is to ask for him. And once he's there, unless you're lucky enough to find a psychic sommelier, you'll need to tell him a few things so he can better help you find a wine you'll love. Be prepared to tell the sommelier …

> What you're all having to eat.
>
> How much you want to spend.
>
> What you have in mind, if you have anything in mind.
>
> What sorts of wines you typically enjoy—red, white, a little sweet, bone-dry—whatever you can think of.

Armed with this information, the sommelier should be able to offer a few different choices that would match the food, your tastes, and your pocketbook, and be able to explain to you why each one would be a good choice.

Quick Sip

If you don't want to say out loud how much you want to spend, then say, "I was thinking about something in this range" while pointing to the price of a bottle on the wine list. A savvy sommelier will get the hint.

What to Do with the Cork

After you've ordered a wine, there's a little routine the wine person will go through before he leaves you alone to enjoy it. This isn't to make him look good, nor to make you embarrassed. It's just to give you the opportunity to make sure the wine he's pulled from the cellar is indeed the one you ordered and that it's in good shape. The routine goes like this:

Check the Label

Before opening the bottle, the wine person will bring the bottle to you and show you the label. This is your chance to make sure he's pulled the right bottle from the cellar. Look to see if …

- It's the right producer.
- It's the right vintage.
- It's the right bottling (if you ordered Chateau Froufrou Reserve, but this one doesn't say Reserve, it's not the same wine).

If any of these elements don't match up, point it out to the sommelier and insist on the bottle you ordered. You have every right to be suspicious if the wine person tries to pass off a different vintage or bottling of a wine without telling you; while it doesn't happen often, it is possible that the bottling you're being offered is cheaper than the one you ordered.

 **Sour Grapes**

If you order a bottle of wine and the waiter comes to your table with it already opened, insist on a new, unopened bottle. How else can you be sure the bottle isn't one they opened yesterday?

Ignore the Cork

When you've verified that the wine the sommelier is about to open is indeed the one you ordered, the sommelier will open it up and place the cork on the table.

What are you supposed to do with it? Nothing. Presenting the cork is a tradition that dates from the early days of bottling wine, when fraud was rampant and it was important to make sure the name on the cork matched that on the label. Winemakers may smell the cork to see if it smells of mold or infection, but normal people like you and me will smell nothing but wet, winey cork. Best to just leave it on the table.

Take a Taste

Now that you've verified the label and ignored the cork, it's time for you to taste the wine. The wine person will pour a little bit into your glass and then stand there, waiting for your okay. He's waiting for you to taste the wine.

Don't be embarrassed. Just give the glass a little swirl, smell the wine, and then taste it. What you're looking to determine is if the wine is sound—that is, that it isn't spoiled in any way. You'll know if it's spoiled if it's …

- **Corked**—A corked wine is one that's been infected with a bacterium called, in short, TCA. Although it's harmless to your health, it makes the wine smell and taste like wet cardboard, or like an old, musty attic.
- **Vinegared**—If the wine smells like vinegar, there's a problem.
- **Bubbling**—If the wine you ordered wasn't sparkling, but the one in your glass is bubbling, then something has gone wrong.

If the wine is any of these things, tell the wine person. He should immediately remove the glass and the wine and get you another bottle. Do not feel guilty about it; the sommelier would much rather have you enjoy the wine you've ordered, and besides, the restaurant will get a refund for the spoiled bottle from the purveyor from which they ordered it.

One caveat: It is *not* okay to send a wine back because you don't like how it tastes. Sometimes a sommelier will take a bottle back on the basis of taste if he's the one who suggested it, but he doesn't have to. And certainly, if you ordered it on your own without asking for help, then you have to take responsibility for your choice of wine. Another reason to ask for help!

Off the Vine

> Doggy bags for wine? It's true: Some states allow you to bring an unfinished bottle of wine home with you, as long as it is firmly sealed before leaving the premises.

Pouring All Around

After you've okayed a wine, the waiter will move on to the next person and fill everyone's glasses, coming back to you last. He'll fill the glasses only half full or less, depending on the size of the glass. This isn't to be cheap, but to allow you room to swirl the wine without getting it on yourself or the tablecloth.

Sometimes waiters pour a little overzealously, hoping that if they can get you to finish the bottle faster, they can sell you another bottle. Don't let them drive. You're the customer, the one who they are supposed to please. Feel free to tell the waiter to slow down, hold off, and let you enjoy the wine at your own speed.

Do-It-Yourself Sommelier-ing

What if you go to a restaurant and there's not a soul on staff who can tell the difference between a white Zinfandel and a red Zinfandel, let alone the differences between the list's 15 Chardonnays? Start thinking like a sommelier.

Food First

The first question any good sommelier will ask you is, "What are you having tonight?" They do that so they can pick wines that will match the food as well as your tastes. In the sommelier-less case, it will also buy you time in making a wine decision.

Some things to keep in mind:

- Match color. It's true that white wines can go with red meat, and red wines can go well with fish, but making them work can be tricky. Better to stick to the "white wine with white meat, red wine with red meat" if you're unsure.

- Weigh the choices. If you're having a steak, would you rather have a light white wine or a hearty red? The red would stand up better to the red meat.

- Feel it out. Some wines are very smooth and velvety, others feel rough (lots of tannin) or tongue-tinglingly tangy (lots of acidity).

Very rich dishes, like foie gras or roast duck, benefit from wines with lots of acidity or tannin; it's as if those components help scrub your tongue clean, readying it for the next rich bite. More delicate dishes, like chicken, often do better next to softer wines.

Think Mechanically

When wine and food combine in a good way, the result can make each taste better than either would on its own. When the match is off, though, it can create a war on your tongue. Keep these guidelines in mind:

- Salt plays up tannin. Salty dishes require less tannic wines.

- Pepper plays up alcohol. Avoid high-octane wines (14 to 16 percent alcohol) with spicy foods.

- Sweetness likes acidity. If the dish has a bit of sweetness in it, look for a wine that has lots of acidity along with a little sweetness. If the wine is low in acidity, the combination will feel heavy and cloying, while if it's very dry, it'll taste unpleasantly dry next to the dish's sweetness.

- Tannin loves protein. If you're ordering a steak, look for a red that has a decent amount of tannin in it. The tannin will bind to protein in the steak instead of your tongue.

Once you've thought about how your dinner choices might affect the wine, you'll have a pretty good idea of what sort of wines you're looking for. The next thing to do is decide how much you want to spend, and then you can go looking for the good deals.

Finding the Good Deals

Every good wine list has its golden spots, the places you'll find better buys in wines than in others. It's just a matter of identifying them. So every time you're handed a wine list, scan the whole thing first and think about the following points.

Find the Emphasis

Does the wine list have an unusually high proportion of Rieslings or wines from Chile? That's usually a sign that the wine buyer thinks those wines have a particular affinity for the restaurant's cuisine, or that he has such a passion for those wines that he can't stop buying them up.

Either way, the mark-up on these wines is often less than it is on other wines, since these are the ones the wine buyer really wants diners to check out.

Avoid the Obvious

Big names are big for a reason. People find them easy to like and easy to buy. If you see big names on a wine list, chances are, it's because the wine buyer knows people want them, not because they are his favorites. Lesser-known names are harder to sell, so the wine buyer will often mark them up less than the wines that sell themselves.

Delve Into the Obscure

Are there wines from Slovenia on the wine list? Or how about Lebanon? Maybe there's a New York State wine and you're in California. If there's a wine that seems unusual on the list, it's often worth a try. Chances are, it's a wine the wine buyer tasted and said, "Wow, I have to have this." And chances are, it's selling for a good price because most people aren't going to buy it without some coaxing.

Stay Away from the Edges

Often the cheapest and most expensive wines on a list serve mostly to hit price points. They are wines that don't need a lot of pushing. Price-sensitive people will play it safe with the cheapest wine, while those interested in impressing will often go for the most expensive.

The middle of the list tends to be the most visited part of the list—it's a sort-of "comfort zone" where diners feel they'll look neither cheap nor extravagant. There may be great buys in there, but for the sweetest spots, look just under or just over that zone. That's the place where the wine buyer has to work a little harder to sell the wines, and that means he's got to feel pretty strongly about them.

To Tip or Not to Tip

Unless you've asked the sommelier to go out of his way for you—say, you brought six bottles, each of which needed to be decanted—there's no need to tip the sommelier separately from the rest of the staff.

However, if you've brought your own wine, make sure to add to the bill what you expect you would have paid for a bottle of wine had you ordered off the list, and tip on that final amount. Even if you didn't pay for it there, it took the same amount of effort on the part of the staff to serve it.

Also a note on the part of restaurant staff across the country. If you've ordered or brought in something really special, a great way to become a favorite guest is to save a glass of wine for the staff. Most restaurant workers can't afford special wines, and they are ever grateful for the chance to try them.

Part 2

Whites: The Big Four

So what are you in the mood for tonight? A rich, creamy Chardonnay, or a bright and perky Sauvignon Blanc? Maybe the mood calls for a Pinot Grigio, or the food is crying out for a tangy Riesling. Of course, there are other white wines out there, but these are the four varieties that dominate the scene. This section lays out what to expect from each one, from flavor to price.

4

Chardonnay

In This Chapter

- Light, crisp, bright Chardonnay
- Tropical powerhouses
- Burgundy's beckoning
- Chardonnay's price points

You've seen it on a zillion wine lists; you've heard it ordered countless times at restaurants, bars, and wine stores. It takes up the most shelf space in almost any wine store because it's Chardonnay, the it-girl of white wines.

How'd she get to be so popular? Take that golden color, for one. Add a bright, citrusy personality; an applelike wholesomeness; tremendous versatility; and a hardiness that allows her to thrive almost anywhere, and it's a no-brainer. She's a great wine to have around. The question is, out of the thousands of bottles, which one do you want?

From Apples to Pineapples

Say it's the end of a long day at work. You meet a friend for something cold, wet, and refreshing before dinner. You could have a beer, but how about a glass of crisp, chilled Chardonnay?

That's great—only it's not quite as easy as simply asking for a glass of Chardonnay. Not all Chardonnays are crisp and refreshing. Some are more like heavy down quilts—great when it's cold out and you want to cuddle up with something warm, soft, and comforting, but not what you're looking for now. To have a good idea of what kind of Chardonnay you're getting, you want to think about ...

- Where it's coming from.
- How it was made.

You can find out where it's from by looking at the label. How it was made might be listed on the back label or can be guessed from price. Read on to find out how these factors affect the wine's taste.

The Importance of Place

You heard it already in Chapter 2, but here it is again. Place matters because the climate of a place makes all the difference to a grape.

Chardonnay has the advantage that it can grow just about anywhere on the planet (so far, there's no Chardonnay on Mars, but just wait). The grape's advantage, though, gives you more to think about:

It can grow in both cool and warm areas, so its flavor will be very different in each.

For instance, in Champagne, France, where Chardonnay makes up a major portion of the vineyards, the weather is typically so cool that the grapes don't get entirely ripe. They're too acidic to make into pleasant-tasting still wine, so the Champenoise add sugar and perform some other tricks that turns the wines into sparkling wine. (More on that in Chapter 14.)

In a warmer place, like California's Central Valley, for example, Chardonnay can become so ripe and sweet it makes wines as tropical as a piña colada.

So when you're thinking about ordering a Chardonnay, think about what you want it to taste like, and see if the flavors that come to mind are more tropical or cool. Then you'll have a good idea of where to look for the Chardonnay you have in mind.

Cool-Climate Chardonnay Havens

If you want a refreshing, light Chardonnay, look for wines from these regions:

- Burgundy, France
- Sonoma Coast, California
- Western Australia
- South Africa

Only one of these places—Burgundy—falls on a high latitude, where it's obviously a bit chilly. The other three regions fall in more temperate zones,

but they are all near ice-cold oceans. The breezes
that come whipping off these cold bodies of water
hold that chill in the air for miles, cooling the
grapes regardless of how strongly the sun shines.
The result is grapes that are fully ripe yet have
plenty of acidity.

Tropical Dreams

Ever have one of those days when you wish you
could disappear to a tropical island? You can. Just
turn up the heat and pour yourself a glass of
Chardonnay—warm-climate Chardonnay, that is.
In many warm places, Chardonnay gets so ripe that
it begins to taste like pineapple, mango, or baked
apples, and there's so little acidity left that the wine
lays on the tongue like a soft, warm blanket.

To find warm-climate Chardonnay, look to these
regions

- Central Coast, California
- Languedoc, France
- South Australia
- Central Valley, Chile
- Mendoza, Argentina

Those five places are only the biggest players. You
can expect warm, ripe Chardonnay from anywhere
else it's warm, like Southern Italy and Texas, too.
See how easy this is?

Mineral Mysteries

Cool, crisp quaffs and tropical fruit bombs sound delicious, but if that was all there was to Chardonnay, the variety wouldn't have such an ardent following or command prices that rise well above $100 a bottle. Great Chardonnay also has *terroir* and *minerality*.

Terroir (tare-*whar*) is a French word that means, loosely, the taste of a place. It's the unique flavor determined by the amount of sun, warmth, wind, and water a grape vine gets, as well as the angle of the slope, the soil, and the plants, animals, and insects that live around it. In short, terroir is everything that affects how the grape vine grows and, therefore, how its fruit tastes. A wine with a sense of terroir is one that tastes like it has come from a particular place, typically a place that has made wine for long enough to establish a reputation for wines that taste a certain way.

Minerality is a term that often goes hand in hand with terroir. It's a taste of the earth, something that's not fruity, but savory and hard to describe. For Chardonnay, the mineral that comes up most often is chalk—which isn't so surprising, considering that the grape vine prefers to grow in chalky, limestone-rich soils. Although scientists haven't been able to prove that the vine sucks up minerals from the soil, sometimes it sure tastes like it.

Great Chardonnays are said to have not just a tasty balance of fruit and acidity, but also intriguing notes of minerals, and even a place-specific flavor.

The most famous Chardonnays are those from Burgundy, France, where the French find the flavor of Chardonnays from one piece of land to another so different that they've broken up the region into nearly 100 different appellations.

Sound confusing? It is, but to many wine lovers, the differences from one appellation's Chardonnays to another's are fascinating, and they'll spend years trying to commit the differences to memory. Considering that the only way to do this is to taste, it's not a bad addiction, if you can afford it.

Burgundy: Worth the Work

Burgundy, France, is the most hallowed region on Earth for Chardonnay. The grape is such a part of life here that any white wine from Burgundy that doesn't have the name of the grape on it is made from Chardonnay.

That makes it sound easy, but unfortunately, it's not quite so simple. Chardonnays from Burgundy not only don't list the grape on the label, but they may not even say "Burgundy" (or *Bourgogne*, in French.)

 Sour Grapes

When you buy a Chardonnay from Burgundy, it won't say "Chardonnay." It may not even say "Burgundy." Instead, it will simply give the name of an appellation; it's up to the buyer to know it's in Burgundy.

Instead, they'll just list an appellation, leaving it to the buyer to know that the appellation is in Burgundy. This requires a little memorization.

Lay of the Land

Bear with me here. Burgundy is a little confusing, but its pleasures are worth the work. The most important thing to understand is that Burgundy is broken down into three districts. They are, from north to south:

- Chablis
- Côte d'Or
- Mâconnais

Chablis's cool climate in combination with a soil high in limestone and ancient oyster shells (it used to be an ocean bed) makes for lean, minerally Chardonnays that seem designed for drinking with oysters on the half shell.

 **Sour Grapes**

> Note that Chablis is the name of a place and the wines from that place. If a wine is labeled Chablis but doesn't come from Chablis, France, it's not the real item.

Côte d'Or, or "Golden Slope," never shows up on wine labels, but the appellations it holds represent the heart of Burgundy. It's typically divided into the

Pinot Noir–heavy Côte de Nuits in the north and the Chardonnay stronghold, Côte de Beaune, to the south. To get a taste of its Chardonnay, look for wines labeled with these regions:

- **St-Aubin**—Simple, earthy
- **Meursault**—Rich, nutty, deeply mineral
- **Puligny-Montrachet**—Cool, steely
- **Chassagne-Montrachet**—Opulent, often expensive

The Mâconnais lies farthest south. Its most important appellations are:

- **Mâcon**—Mostly simple, medium-bodied Chardonnays (and a few outstanding, more complex examples)
- **Pouilly-Fuissé**—Rich, mineral-laden Chardonnays
- **St-Veran**—Between Mâcon and Pouilly-Fuissé in richness and minerality

There's one more thing: Burgundians are so serious about their wines that not only have they broken down the region into a hundred appellations, but they also have selected 561 vineyards as Premier Cru and another 33 as the even more prestigious Grand Cru. These vineyards are so highly regarded that they often appear solo on the wine label, without any reference to their designation. You could memorize them, but there's little need. The high prices make their status clear.

California's Liquid Sun

France isn't the only country to make Chardonnay with distinct regional differences; California does, too. It's no surprise, considering that Chardonnay is the most planted wine grape, growing from as far south as Temecula all the way up to Mendocino.

Although much of the state's production comes from the warm, sunny Central Valley, where Chardonnay grows fat, sweet, and affordable, more interesting Chardonnay comes from cooler corners, where climate, altitude, wind, and/or fog protect the grapes from heat. Here are some of the regions that excel in Chardonnay:

- **Sonoma County** sprawls from the mountains out to the ocean, so it's tough to generalize, but the subregions Sonoma Coast, Dry Creek Valley, Russian River Valley, and Chalk Hill stand out for Chardonnay.

- **Carneros** sits at the northern tip of San Francisco Bay, straddling both Napa and Sonoma counties. The bay channels cool breezes and fog up onto the land, cooling the vines and making for a long, even growing season that allows Chardonnay to retain its acidity even as it gets sweetly ripe.

- **Edna Valley** makes the best of the cool winds off Morro Bay, to produce lean, citrusy Chardonnay.

Of course, region isn't the sole determinant of a Chardonnay style. The winemaker also has a say.

Butter, Vanilla, or Nuts, Anyone?

Regardless of where Chardonnay grows, the wine-maker has the final say in how the wine is going to taste. Does he want it to be light and pure, or rich and creamy? Will it taste of fruit, or of buttered toast, or of yeast or minerals?

Why do you care? Because if you know how these flavors come about, you have a better chance of finding the sort of Chardonnay that you want. Here are three things that you'll want to know:

- Was it oaked?
- Did it go through malolactic fermentation?
- Did it spend time on the lees?

Sometimes the back label will answer these questions, but more often than not, you'll have to ask someone who's tasted the wine how it tastes.

Oak

You can make wine in a cement tank, a plastic tub, a bathtub, or even a shoe, but the two most popular containers are stainless-steel tanks and oak barrels.

Stainless steel is preferred for some Chardonnay because it is inert—that is, it adds no flavor of its own to the wine. Steel also can be chilled, which helps keep the wine inside bright and fresh.

Oak barrels, on the other hand, can add a host of flavors to a wine, if the barrels are relatively new. (Like tea bags, the longer they're used, the more

flavor is leached out, until there's nothing left.)
Most notable among oak's flavors are these:

- Wood
- Vanilla, coconut, spice
- Smoke or toast

Wood, vanilla, coconut, and spice come from com-
pounds in the oak that leach into the wine. In general, the more time the wine spent in contact with
oak and/or the younger the oak barrels are, the
stronger the oak flavors. After about three years, an
oak barrel won't have much flavor left to give.

Smoke and toast are flavors that come from the
toasted insides of the barrels. When a cooper (the
person who builds the barrels) makes a barrel, he
chars the inside of it over a fire before he puts the
top on. How long he lets it toast depends on how
much toasty flavor the vintner wants to give the
wine; vintners can request light, medium, or heavy
toast.

About a decade ago, winemakers went a little oak
barrel-crazy, and for a while Chardonnay often
tasted more like oak than fruit. Today most vintners exercise restraint, making wines that have fruit
flavors bolstered, not masked, by oak. Still, it's so
common for Chardonnay to have oak flavors that
many producers now mark unoaked Chardonnays
as such right on the label. So if you want a Chardonnay that tastes purely of the fruit, free of oak
influence, look for those that say "Unoaked."

Off the Vine

Barrels are expensive; top-of-the-line models can run $800 and up. So how do those $6 Chardonnays get their oaky vanilla flavors? Often, from planks of oak or bags of oak chips or sawdust that soak in the tank of wine just like teabags until the desired degree of oaky flavor is achieved.

Creamsicles and Rising Bread

Ever have a Chardonnay that tasted as smooth and heavy as cream, with maybe even a slightly milky flavor? It probably went through malolactic fermentation, or ML, in wine geek-speak. This is a secondary fermentation whereby hard-feeling malic acid (think of green apples) is transformed into gentler lactic acid (think milk).

For white wines, ML is an option. Some winemakers encourage it; other winemakers prefer the tarter, leaner flavors of a wine that hasn't gone through ML. Often winemakers combine a batch of wine that went through ML with a portion that didn't in order to achieve a balance between tartness and creamy textures. How can you tell if a white wine has gone through ML before you buy it? You can't, unless the winemaker has noted it in the informational blurb on the back label, or someone knowledgeable about that particular wine can tell you so.

Otherwise, you won't know it until you taste it—
and if it's done well, even then you won't notice.
It'll simply taste good and feel delicious.

For most red wines, ML is imperative. Without it
they'd be unpleasantly hard, even sharp, especially
if the wine is also tannic.

Another way to get a creamy feel and add extra flavor is to stir the lees. *Lees* are the dead yeast cells,
miniscule particles of grapes, and other sediment
that settles out of a wine after it's fermented. Vintners who are looking to make a rich, complexly fla-
vored Chardonnay often leave the lees in the barrel
with the wine and stir them up from the bottom
every so often. The resulting Chardonnay tends to
have complex flavors, including a rich, yeasty character reminiscent of rising bread and a smooth (but
not milky) texture.

Winespeak

Lees are miniscule particles of grapes,
yeast, and other sediment that settle out
of a wine after it's fermented. Many vintners stir up the lees to give Chardonnay
extra flavor.

What Money Buys

You can get a decent Chardonnay for $2.99 or
$299. Where the decimal point falls depends on
the yield of the vineyard, the length of time the

wine was kept at the winery before being sold, the cost of oak barrels, and, of course, the less tangible but very real reputation of the vintner and vineyard.

For instance, at $30 or more, you can pretty much expect that the winemaker pulled the grapes from a low-yielding, high-quality vineyard and then treated those grapes to a long, slow fermentation and aging on oak, and didn't rush the bottled wine to the market. The vintner's goal, in this case, is to release a wine that has concentration, complexity, and, most likely, an ability to get better with a few more years of age. It's a wine for special occasions, rich food, or the wine cellar.

Quick Sip

Chardonnay bargains:

- Beringer
- Echelon
- Edna Valley Vineyard
- Pepperwood Grove

A wine under $15 would be entirely different. The object of the vintner is typically to make an easy-drinking, quality Chardonnay to drink now, tonight, on its own or with casual food. Chardonnays, $15 and under, are the wines to look for when you just want to have something on hand to drink during the week or when friends drop by.

Chapter 5

Sauvignon Blanc

In This Chapter

- Lean and green Sauvignon Blanc
- Liquid minerals
- The dirt on Fumé Blanc
- When to drink Sauvignon Blanc

If Chardonnay is the it-girl of white grapes, then Sauvignon is the rebel, different in almost every way. Where Chardonnay is fat and round, Sauvignon is slim and sharp. Where Chardonnay is easy to say, Sauvignon takes a little more French 101. Where Chardonnay is easy-going, Sauvignon Blanc gives the grape grower a little more trouble. But, of course, these differences are some of the things that make it so interesting. Read on to see what I mean.

The Flavor of Green

Want to taste tart? Pull a Sauvignon Blanc berry from a vine. Its firm skin and greenish cast right away suggest that it's going to be more crisp than tender, more acid than sweet. Taste it: There's the taste of green. Depending on where it grew, green could mean grass, herbs, or veggies, or it could mean sweet-tart gooseberries and juicy green plums. At the ripest end of the spectrum, it could be honeydew melon. Which one's for you? Where do you find them? All over the world, but most especially here:

- France's Loire Valley
- New Zealand
- California

Each region has its own particular style. Get to know the regions, and you'll be able to pick and choose to your liking.

Lean, Lithe, Powerful Whites

Let's take an armchair trip to the Loire. We'll drive about four hours south from Paris and head to the mouth of the Loire River, where it dumps into the Atlantic Ocean. That wind whipping off the water is pretty darn cold, and the gray skies do nothing much to warm us up. We trudge up river, leaving behind the icy beds that make a home for some of the best oysters in the world. The banks get more hilly and the bone-cutting cold loses its edge, but it still ain't warm. It's here, some 200 miles inland, that Sauvignon Blanc calls its home.

Quick Sip

Loire Sauvignon Blancs are labeled by place, not grape, so when you hanker for a cool, chalky, mineral-tinged Sauvignon, look for wines from these places:

- **Menetou-Salon:** The gentlest Loire Sauvignon
- **Quincy:** Crisp and chalky
- **Pouilly-Fumé:** Slightly smoky (fumé) Sauvignon
- **Reuilly:** Hard to find, but often well priced; very much like the wines from nearby Quincy
- **Sancerre:** Smoky, flinty, with cold, grassy, grapefruit-like flavors

Sauvignon Blanc doesn't mind that chill in the air; in fact, it likes it. The cool temps allow the grapes to get ripe, but not so much they'll lose their zingy acidity. A Loire Sauvignon Blanc, by definition, is a nervy white wine, ready to pierce a plump oyster or cut through a sausage nested in sauerkraut.

Also important is the soil, so full of limestone that caves pock the hills, some of which have been turned into wine cellars since they stay so nice and cool year-round. The Sauvignon Blanc of the Loire Valley is noted for its chalky minerality, and chalk is a form of limestone. Great Loire wine, in fact, tastes more like cold, chalky stone, smoky flint, or grass than fruit—a good thing in the eyes of terroirists, oyster-lovers, and folks who appreciate restrained white wines.

Off the Vine

Sauvignon Blanc also grows in Bordeaux, France, just south of the Loire by a couple of hours. Here, however, it's typically blended with Sémillon, a white grape with rich, waxy flavors. The combination of the two makes for some of the most sophisticated, long-lived Sauvignon Blanc blends in the world— and you'll pay for them. Lynch-Bages and Haut-Brion are two names to check out.

The Loire may have been the first region to take Sauvignon Blanc to fame and fortune, but there's another place that's only lately come onto the scene—New Zealand.

Cat Pee on a Gooseberry Bush?

It's a joke, but it's not far from the truth: Cat Pee on a Gooseberry Bush is really the name of a New Zealand Sauvignon Blanc. Even if you've never smelled that combination, it gives you a clear idea of the style—head-turningly pungent and strong.

Why's it so different that the Sauvignon Blanc of the Loire? Blame Mother Nature and a whole lot of uncontrollable influences, but then turn your attention to the things we do know. For one, most parts of New Zealand are a heck of a lot sunnier than France's Loire Valley, allowing the grapes to get riper, rounder, more full of fruit flavor. Add to that younger vines: the New Zealand wine industry is only about 30 years old (many vintners think that older vines give more concentrated, soil-driven flavors).

Quick Sip

New Zealand Sauvignon Blanc will always list the grape on the label. The most famous examples come from the Marlborough region and run $10 to $20; look for names like Babich, Kim Crawford, Nautilus, Stoneleigh, Villa Maria, and Wairau River.

New Zealanders also tend to like to make their Sauvignon Blanc in stainless-steel tanks, where they can keep the juice cold and clean, preserving every iota of freshness and fruit. Unlike many Loire Sauvignon Blancs, which can be aged to good effect, New Zealand Sauvignon Blanc is, in most cases, made to be drunk straight away. Its bright, limey, grassy flavors make it fabulous at beach barbecues, with grilled shrimp and fish, and its green flavors have a penchant for matching well with vegetables, even those like asparagus and artichokes in vinaigrette.

If New Zealand Sauvignon Blanc is too much for the occasion, though, you might want to try an example from California.

California

Want a Sauvignon Blanc that's less pungent than New Zealand's, with fewer sharp edges than the Loire's? Try California, where the sun seems to seep into the Sauvignon Blanc grapes, making for riper and rounder versions of its wine.

Quick Sip _____

Screamin' Sauvignon bargains ($15 or less):

- Morandé, Veramonte (Chile)
- Hess, Kenwood, Kunde, Joel Gott, Mason (California)
- Buitenverwachting, Neil Ellis, Kanu (South Africa)

Though no one particular region in California stands out for Sauvignon Blanc, Sonoma and Napa valleys claim most of the state's best, the cooler regions of both striking a balance between the grape's herbal characters and its richer, melon-ball side. If you prefer leaner, greener Sauvignon Blanc, look to Santa Ynez and Monterey; for more lush styles, look to Santa Barbara.

The Story Behind Fumé Blanc

Fumé Blanc is the same thing as Sauvignon Blanc. You can blame Robert Mondavi for the confusion: Back in the 1960s, when Sauvignon Blanc wasn't so popular, Mondavi began making Sauvignon Blanc in oak barrels, which gave it a richer, smoky taste. Eventually, he renamed the wine Fumé Blanc, a play on France's famous Sauvignon Blanc wine region, Pouilly-Fumé.

The name is now used by many wineries throughout California, although some of the wines never saw the inside of an oak barrel. So when you're looking for a smoky, oak-aged Sauvignon Blanc, it's best to ask if the Fumé Blanc you're looking at is indeed oak aged.

Southern Sauvignon Blanc

The Loire Valley, New Zealand, and California don't hold the corner of the market on Sauvignon Blanc; good examples are available from regions all over the world. In particular, you might want to check out those from the following regions:

- **Casablanca, Chile**—In this high-altitude region north of Santiago, Sauvignon Blanc soaks up the sun while staying cool in the thin air. The result is Sauvignon Blanc with a rich, green figginess and bright acidity.
- **Stellenbosch and Constantia, South Africa**—This is the closest the new world comes to Loire Sauvignon Blanc, with a salt-air freshness and cool minerality.

- **Australia**—This country is a gold mine of affordable, quaffable Sauvignon Blanc, many blended with Sémillon, another French-born white wine grape, to make easy-drinking, fruity wines from $7 to $10.

Quick Sip

Sauvignon splurges:

- Sancerre from Cotat, Mellot, and Reverdy
- Pouilly-Fumé from Cailbourdin, Didier Dageneau, Ladoucette
- California versions from Araujo, Cakebread, Dry Creek Vineyards, Peter Michael

When to Drink Sauvignon Blanc

Vegetarians and vegetable lovers, listen up. Sauvignon Blanc is one of your best friends when it comes to pairing wine and food. There's something about its green, herbal flavors and bright acidity that makes it match brilliantly with everything from salads to hard-to-pair vegetables like asparagus and artichokes.

It's also a wine that's terrific to have on hand for fish and light meats, since it's generally light and lean. Rarely will you find an example that's so strong it could stand up to red meat.

Chapter 6

Riesling

In This Chapter

- Riesling's versatility
- Where to find the best
- Parsing German labels
- How wonderfully affordable Riesling is

When James Joyce said "White wine is electricity," he must have been referring to Riesling. The white wines from this grape throw sparks, they are so bright and acidic. That acidity makes the wine food's best friend, as it can spear a French fry as cleanly as it does a poached fish. If only it weren't so picky about where it lives ....

Acid Dreams and Hard Rocks

Riesling might be the most versatile white-wine grape in the world when it comes to the variety of wines it can produce. Depending on where it's grown and when it's picked, its flavors can range from lime pith to chin-dripping peaches, from bone dry to syrup sweet. All great Rieslings have two elements in common: acidity and minerality.

Acidity functions like a backbone for a wine's flavors. In Riesling, it acts to keep them firm yet lifted, light on the tongue no matter how substantial. Riesling is like a long-distance runner: lean, lithe, and light, yet strong and built for endurance.

Quick Sip _____

Confused by the idea of "minerality" in wines? Taste different mineral waters side by side, smell a wet blackboard, crumble some limestone, rub a rusty cast-iron fence (carefully), and go outside after a rain and try to describe the scent. You may or may not find these same scents in wines, but you'll get the idea of minerality.

Maybe it's because Riesling's flavors are typically so light and clear, but it seems like Riesling vines have an exceptional ability to pull flavor from the ground. Great Riesling often has a mineral flavor like wet slate; cold, hard stones; or even oil or gasoline. It might sound weird, but that minerality is an element many Riesling lovers search out because it adds something unique to the wine, a taste of the place from which it came.

If Riesling gets too ripe too quickly, though, as it does in many parts of California, for instance, then the grape's fruit flavors dominate without enough acidity or minerality to make them interesting. Riesling likes it cold and stony, as in these regions:

- Germany
- Alsace, France
- Austria
- New York State

Four places might not seem like many, but read on to see the tremendous array of choices that await in the Riesling aisle.

Germany

When it comes to Riesling, Germany holds the crown. It nearly lost it in the 1970s, when sweet, soft wines like Blue Nun flooded the market, but today, the country's wines are once again turning heads. They aren't all sweet; in fact, many are bone dry. To know what you're getting here, you have to learn something called the Prädikat.

How Sweet It Is

The Prädikat (prah-de-*khat*) is a German measure of how ripe the grapes were at harvest, which, in turn, can give you an idea of the sweetness of the wine. There are five levels of Prädikat, each signifying riper grapes:

1. Kabinett (ka-bee-*net*)
2. Spätlese (*spate*-laze-uh)
3. Auslese (*aows*-laze-uh)
4. Beerenauslese (beer-en-*aows*-laze-uh, or just BA)
5. Trockenbeerenauslese (*trok*-en-*beer*-en-*aows*-laze-uh, or TBA)

Here's the catch: Sweet grapes don't necessarily make sweet wine. You could have Auslese-level grapes but decide to let the wine ferment until there is no sugar left, thereby making a dry wine.

It is admittedly confusing, even to the Germans, but in the end, there are two things you can bet on:

BA and TBA are always dessert sweet; Auslese are, too, 98 percent of the time.

Anything with the word *trocken* (dry) on the label will be stone dry, regardless of the Prädikat. And even though "halbtrocken" means half-dry, it also signifies a dry wine.

So if you're looking for a dry German Riesling to serve with dinner, look for one that says Kabinett, Spätlese, or trocken.

Now that we're clear on the Prädikat, it's time to delve into the regional differences.

Off the Vine

Many wine snobs equate sweetness with cheapness, as in White Zinfandel. In German Riesling, however, a little sweetness can be your friend, taking the edge off the grape's sharp acidity and stony minerality. Also, in combination with the wine's low alcohol, that sweet edge can help combat the hot-pepper heat of Szechuan chicken and other spicy dishes. So when it comes to German Riesling, don't let a little sweetness scare you away.

Geographic Variations

Every winegrowing region of Germany makes Riesling—which makes remembering what Germany excels at simple, but leads to confusion when you realize that each region has its own style. Realize however, that the styles are simply reflections of the soil and climate in each region, and it's not so hard. For example:

- **Mosel-Saar-Ruwer** is known for Rieslings as dramatic as the sheer slate slopes that rise above the hairpin curves of the Mosel River, with cold, stony flavors and vibrant acidity.

- **Nahe**'s intricate mix of soils makes for softer Rieslings with earthy flavors.

- **Rheingau**'s sun-warmed south-facing slopes and cold slate soils make for dry, powerful Rieslings, which are often more fruity than Mosel's.

- **Franken**'s southerly situation makes for soft, fruity Rieslings, which are immediately recognizable by their squat, round bottles (called a *Bocksbeutel*).

- **Pfalz**'s flat, warm countryside turns out ripe and peachy Rieslings with softer acidity than the Mosel's.

Quick Sip

Riesling names to look for:
- Dr. Loosen, Selbach-Oster (Mosel)
- Diel, Dönhoff (Nahe)
- Leitz, Robert Weil (Rheingau)
- Fürst, Schmitts Kinder (Franken)
- Müller-Catoir, Lingenfelder (Pfalz)

Now that you know how to parse a German wine label, Gothic script be damned, you have access to many of the world's greatest Rieslings. However, there are a few more you should try.

The Franco-German Connection

Follow the Rhine River south from Germany's Pfalz region, and you'll end up in Alsace, France. Historically, Alsace became a part of France in only 1648, and it's been occupied by Germany twice in the past hundred years, so it's no surprise that the major grape here is Riesling, as it is in Germany. Alsace is also one of the few places in France that labels its wines with the name of the grape when it's 100 percent of a single variety—like Germans do.

Quick Sip

Outstanding names in Alsace:
- Zind-Humbrecht
- Marcel Deiss
- Domaine Weinbach

However, the similarities end there. Alsace's climate is cool like Germany's Mosel, but its vineyards are in one of France's sunniest spots, protected as they are from rain and clouds by the Vosges Mountains. The combination of cool temperatures and long hours of sun allow the grapes to ripen slowly and abundantly without losing acidity, making for some of the most turbo-charged Riesling on the planet. In addition, Alsace vintners like to ferment their Rieslings until they are bone dry. So, you want Riesling for a hearty choucroute? Alsace grows it.

Just be prepared to pay: The most impressive versions run $20 and up.

Austria's Pride

Austria's winegrowing area is small, but it's a powerhouse when it comes to Riesling. The best vineyards are clustered in the east of the country, following the Danube from just west of Vienna to the borders with Hungary. Warmer than Germany's Mosel, Austria's Riesling tends to fall between Mosel and Alsace Riesling in style. The best versions come from three close-together regions:

- Wachau (va-*khow*)
- Kremstal
- Kamptal

In general, the Wachau is the coolest of the three regions, which means it tends to have the most steely, mineral-laden wines. Wines from the Kremstal and Kamptal are nearly identical in flavor; expect them to be more plush in fruit and earth than the Wachau's.

There's another difference between German and Austrian Riesling: Austrians tend to vinify all their Rieslings until they are stone dry. That means there's no Prädikat to worry about. There's just one little system to learn, and it applies only to the wines of the Wachau.

Quick Sip

Awesome Austrians:

- Wachau: Alzinger, Pichler, Prager,
- Kremstal: Nigl, Salomon
- Kamptal: Bründlmayer, Schloss Gobelsburg, Hirsch

Wachau Variations

Wachau vintners label their wines with designations that indicate how ripe the grapes were when they were picked. Since all Wachau Riesling are dry, these designations give the buyer an idea of how powerful the wine will be. In ascending order, the designations are as follows:

- **Steinfeder**—The lightest, rarely seen in the United States, meant for quaffing by the carafe.

- **Federspiel**—Typically meant to be drunk within one to three years; most are light enough to fit best with light vegetable and fish dishes.

- **Smaragd**—Impressive, powerful wines meant for rich food, like bacon-wrapped monkfish, schnitzel, or pork loin, or for cellaring.

Generally, when you're looking for an easy-drinking Riesling to drink tonight, look for a Federspiel-level wine, or anything under $15. Special occasions and cellar space warrant spending the $20 to $80 for a Smaragd.

New York's Little Mosel

For years, American vintners tried in vain to make a decent Riesling. A few have popped up in California and Washington, but nothing to match those from New York State. There, in the Finger Lakes District, along the shist-covered shores of the Cayuga and Seneca lakes, vintners make Rieslings remarkably like Germany's—lean, crisp, and stony. The only problem is that the region is small and young, so the wines can be hard to find.

Quick Sip

Names to look for in NYS Riesling:

- Konstantin Frank
- Standing Stone
- Hermann J. Weimer

What Money Buys

If you want bang for your buck, hang out in the Riesling aisle. Many people fear that Riesling will be sweet; others are scared away by the Germanic text on so many labels. You, however, know how to parse the labels and know that a little sweetness can be an excellent complement to Riesling, especially if you're having spicy Floribbean or Asian cuisine. So dive in.

In general, the difference money buys when it comes to Riesling is complexity and ability to age. Complexity is your call; some people like complex wines all the time, but if you're looking for something simple to sip while preparing dinner, most people would say there's little need for complexity. Riesling running from $7 to $15 tends to offer plenty of bright, limey fruit with some stony notes.

More than $15 brings you into the realm of seriously impressive Riesling, the sort you might pull out for a special dinner of richer fish or white meat. Or if you're into cellaring, this is a goldmine. Riesling's high acidity allows it to age exceptionally well, taking on deeper, richer mineral notes, some developing an oddly appealing "petrol" (fancy for "gasoline") note. "Old" in German Riesling standards is 20 years or more; at 10, a good wine is just warming up.

Either way you go, for dry Riesling, you'll have a hard time spending more than $80—and you'll find plenty of excellent values under $15.

Chapter 7

Pinot Grigio

In This Chapter

- Pinot Grigio's multiple identities
- Snappy styles
- Lush versions
- Pinot's brother, Bianco

Pinot Grigio is the pleasure grape, the one that captures *la dolce vita* of Italy like no other and can also feel like a satin wrap. Whether you're looking for a soft, easy quaff, a sort of Muzak in your glass, or a lush, hedonistic pour, Pinot Grigio can offer it all. You just have to know where to look, and I'll show you in this chapter.

Degrees of Gris

Whether it's called Pinot Grigio, Pinot Gris, Tokay Pinot Gris, or Grauburgunder, it's all the same grape. The differences are the language spoken in the country where it's grown—and the different names are also tip-offs to different styles. In general, here's what you can expect:

- **Pinot Grigio**—The Italian name typically signifies a light and fresh style.
- **Pinot Gris, Tokay Pinot Gris**—These French names are tip-offs to lush, satiny examples.
- **Grauburgunder**—The German name for rich and fruity Germanic versions.

> **Off the Vine**
>
> Gris, grigio, and grau all mean "gray," a reference to the slightly smoky, pink-gray cast of the grape's skin. Some Pinot Grigio wines even have a slightly pink hue.

To understand why different styles are associated with different countries, it helps to know a little bit about where Pinot Grigio excels. Its strongholds are northern Italy, Alsace, and Oregon, with some good examples coming out of Italy's border countries, Austria and Slovenia.

La Dolce Vita

Italy is the most famous producer of Pinot Grigio. Pinot drinkers love the Italianate version for the taste of *la dolce vita* it offers: It's simple, giving, and easy to drink, requiring nothing of its drinker but an open mouth. Sure, its pear and hazelnut flavors whet the appetite with their deliciousness, and its light, refreshing acidity makes it a good pour on its own or with salads. But its real strength is its ability to transfer just enough delicious flavors to please but not interrupt the conversation.

Quick Sip

Party Pinot Grigio for under $15:

- Mezza Corona (Trentino)
- Peter Zemmer (Alto Adige)
- Kris (Veneto)
- Alois Lageder (Alto Adige)
- Pighin (Veneto)

Most of these simple, clean, refreshing versions come from Italy's Veneto, where the rolling terrain is fertile enough to provide plenty of wine to cool the tourists who gather along the shores of Lake Garda every summer.

A little harder to find, but worth the search and the extra money they might ask, are the crisp, almond-toned, pear-filled versions from Friuli and Trentino-Alto Adige.

Friuli's Exceptional Grigio

Some of the best Pinot Grigios come from Friuli. That's because, squashed between the snow-capped Alps and the Gulf of Venice, it's chilly up there. That chill in the air allows Pinot Grigio grapes to hold on to their delicate acidity, while the sun shines enough to ripen them. The result is Pinot Grigio that has the fruity succulence of a cold, crisp pear.

> **Off the Vine**
>
> The Italians might not like to admit it, but many of their best Pinot Grigio vineyards lie over the border from Friuli, in Slovenia. Some Slovenian companies make great Pinot Grigio of their own: Look for Movia, Radikon, and Edi Simcic.

Wines that say "Collio" or "Colli Orientali del Friuli" are from smaller regions within Friuli and share similarly zingy acidity and bright flavors. If you like Friuli's vivacious style of Pinot Grigio, you might also want to check out the wines of nearby Trentino-Alto Adige.

The Adige's Effect

So much of learning about wine is learning about geography. Take Trentino-Alto Adige—it's a mouthful, right? But break it down and it's easy:

The region is just west of Friuli and borders Austria—so we're talking cool, right? The Adige is a river, and *Alto* means "high." Therefore, the Alto Adige is the land at the north end of the river, bordering Austria. In fact, sometimes you'll see wines labeled "Südtiroler," the Germanic term for the area.

In addition to the area's northerly position, add the cool temperatures of high-altitude slopes, and you've got serious chill. That means crisp, acidic wine, similar to Friuli's, but often even more delicate because, of course, the grapes don't get quite as ripe.

Trentino, on the other hand, is the lower end of the region, where it's flatter and warmer. Trentino Pinot Grigio, therefore, has a little more body and little less acidity than Alto Adige. If you want really rich Pinot Grigio, though, you'll have to cross the border into France.

La Vie Gris

There's only one place in France that makes Pinot Grigio, and that's Alsace—here, though, they call it by its French name, Pinot Gris. It's some of the most impressive Pinot Gris in the world—and it's easy to find because, unlike the rest of France, Alsace lists grape varieties on its wine labels.

However, before you go running out to the store, know this: Pinot Gris from Alsace is entirely different than Italy's crisp white versions. In Alsace, it's all about lush. Its satin texture is laden with marzipan-rich flavors of almonds and chin-drippingly-ripe pears.

Quick Sip

Eminence Gris of Gris:

- Adelsheim Vineyards (Oregon)
- Chehalem (Oregon)
- Polz (Austria)
- Domaines Schlumberger (Alsace)
- Trimbach (Alsace)

At its simplest (around the $8 to $12 mark), Alsace's Pinot Gris offers a lot of wine for the money. It has a rich, waxy texture typically laden with dry honey and pear flavors. Pinot Gris is a terrific alternative to Chardonnay when you're looking for a wine that's rich yet free of the weight and sweetness of oak that's so common to Chardonnay in this price range.

Pay more, and you'll get more. The best Pinot Gris in Alsace seem to soak up not only the sun from their bright, protected perch next to the Vosges Mountains, but also the soil's minerality, which gives these wines extra weight and gravitas. The best versions can age for years, turning richer and spicier with time.

Oregon's Stealth Wine

It might sound like a dubious claim to fame, but it's no small feat: Oregon is America's pre-eminent producer of Pinot Gris. Sure, California produces some good, light, fresh Pinot Grigio and a handful of richer styles labeled Pinot Gris, but if you want the best Pinot Gris America has to offer, head straight for Oregon.

Depending on where and how it's made, Oregon Pinot Gris can be light, crisp, and mineral (not unlike Italy's, but with a little more weight and flavor), or rich and spicy, with nutty, honeyed pear flavors.

To know which style of wine is in the bottle, you'll have to read the back label, or just look at the price. Light, everyday wines sell for everyday prices ($10, give or take $3), while Pinot Gris fit for King Salmon or trout crusted with crushed hazelnuts can run into the $20s.

Bianco, Grigio's Brother

While looking for Pinot Grigio, you might find some wines labeled Pinot Bianco (*pee*-no bee-*ahn*-ko). It's not a typo, or the work of a color-blind vintner, but the wine of a grape that's closely related to Pinot Grigio. The wines of this pale-skinned Pinot make for pale white wines that often have a little less flavor than Pinot Grigio. What they lack in flavor, though, they make up for in smooth, silky texture, which can provide a luxurious background for delicate dishes like sautéed white fish.

Alsace grows some Pinot Bianco, too, but the French call it Pinot Blanc (*pee*-no blahnk). As with Pinot Gris, Pinot Blanc grown in Alsace is even richer than its Italian counterpart.

Grigio's Other Outposts

Because Pinot Grigio is so well loved in both its light-and-easy and richly opulent forms, wineries all over the world have planted it. You'll find some good examples coming out of California as well as Australia and New Zealand, and even Argentina has recently gotten in on the game.

Figuring out what style of Pinot Grigio is in the bottle, though, isn't easy. Many wineries use "gris" instead of "grigio" to suggest a richer, fuller style of wine, but it's not always the case.

A better indication of style is often price: Pinot Grigio is one of those grapes that can produce lots of decent juice, but to be inspired, it needs low yields. So, as a general rule of thumb, this is what you can expect:

- **For $12 or less**—A light, summery white wine, perfect for aperitifs, salads, and fried foods, like fritto misto.

- **For $12 to $20**—Pinot Grigio with more guts, whether in acid or fruit richness, the sorts of wines that would stand up to a pork chop or fat pillows of pumpkin-filled ravioli.

- **Above $20**—Opulent Pinot Gris, ready for pâtés or a crown roast of pork, or a decade in the cellar to become even richer and more opulent with age.

Remember Pinot Grigio's brother, Bianco, too. Because it's lesser known, it's often cheaper, which means it can be a good buy.

Part 3

Reds: The Big Five

By now we've covered buttery Chardonnay, grassy Sauvignon Blanc, zingy Riesling, and pear-scented Pinot Grigio, so you're pretty well informed when you're in need of a white wine. How about when there's beef on the menu, or when it's cold outside? In this section, we'll cover the five most-mentioned red varieties out there: Cabernet Sauvignon, Merlot, Pinot Noir, Syrah, and Zinfandel.

Cabernet Sauvignon

In This Chapter

- Cabernet's regal flavors
- Bordeaux, Cabernet's kingdom
- California's great Cabernet
- Cabernet Sauvignon's dad, Franc

If Chardonnay is queen of the white wine world, then Cabernet Sauvignon is king of the reds. Some would even say Cabernet Sauvignon has a regal flavor, with a fruitiness that rarely goes overboard. The variety is marked by sweet-tangy black-fruit flavors, like black currants or blackberries, reined in by tannins and savory herbal notes. The best Cabs age for decades, and the rest are delicious straight away. Where do they come from? All over the world, but to really get to know the variety, you ought to start in France.

Bordeaux's Noble Reds

The first Cabernet Sauvignon wines to gain recognition came from Bordeaux, a vine-filled region on France's western edge that follows the Gironde River from its mouth down to the port town of Bordeaux and a little beyond.

Cabernet loves living here, particularly on the Left Bank, as it's known, between the river and the sea. Here the Atlantic sends cool breezes over the vines in the summer and tempers winter's chill so the vines don't freeze to death.

Off the Vine

Although Cabernet makes up the most of the wines in Bordeaux's Left Bank, vintners often blend in a little Merlot, for its plump richness, as well as small bits of Petit Verdot, Malbec, Carmenère, and Cabernet Franc, which add extra complexity to the flavors and aromas of the wine.

The Left Bank also has lots of gravel, important since Cabernet hates to have cold, wet feet. The gravel quickly percolates water down away from the vine's trunk and keeps the vines warm by absorbing the sun's heat. For Cabernet Sauvignon, this is heaven, and it demonstrates its pleasure in deep, gravelly tasting red wines.

Finding Cabernet-Based Bordeaux

Like most French regions, Bordeaux doesn't feature grape varieties on the label. Instead, it offers only the name of an appellation. So, when you want Cabernet-based Bordeaux, you need to know the appellations of the Left Bank. The most general Left Bank appellations are these:

- Graves
- Haut-Médoc
- Médoc

Wines from these large areas tend to be fairly light, though still tannic enough for a steak. They are usually meant for drinking right away or within the next few years. Most run less than $20.

The sort of Bordeaux that's made Cabernet Sauvignon so sought after comes from smaller areas within these appellations, areas defined for the particular character they give the wine. In general, these are the appellations to look for and what to expect:

- **Listrac-Médoc**—Angular and black-fruited
- **Margaux**—The gentlest of the Left Bank wines, rose-scented with soft black-fruit flavors
- **Moulis**—Firm yet succulently fruity
- **Pauillac**—Big, brooding, tannin-filled monsters
- **Pessac-Léognan**—Smoky, mineral-laden Cabernet
- **St-Éstephe**—Austere, hard, lean reds

- **St-Julien**—Graceful, firm yet friendly Cabernet

These appellations hold some of the most esteemed Cabernet Sauvignon in the world, but even within these smaller appellations, all vineyards aren't considered equal. The Bordelais have classified many of the estates within these appellations according to a scheme cooked up in 1855—thus the frequently heard moniker 1855 Classification.

Class Distinction

In the 1855 Classification, the wines that fetched the highest prices at the time were deemed Premier Cru, or "first growth." The next-highest rank was Deuxième Growth, or "second growth," and so on down the line to fifth growth.

These rankings still hold today, even though many of the estates have changed a lot since they were classified. Only one winery in the history of the classification has changed ranks: Château Mouton-Rothschild was promoted to a first growth in 1973. Nonetheless, the wineries at the top level still tend to bring in the highest prices. Often the quality of their wines warrants it, but it's no guarantee.

Also many wineries that didn't make the classification are now making wines that are better than some of the classed growths. Don't be afraid to look outside the classified estates for great wines: They do exist.

It's also worth looking outside of Bordeaux for great Cabernet, especially in California.

 **Sour Grapes**

In Bordeaux, Premier Cru is the highest rank a wine can achieve, unlike in Burgundy, where Premier Cru is second to Grand Cru, its highest rank. Know also that most Bordeaux estates that rank lower than second growth don't bother to specify rank on their wine label; they'll just leave it at "Grand Cru Classé."

California's Cabernet Sauvignon

Cabernet Sauvignon is California's most planted red wine grape, and after you taste it, you'll know why. From light, herb-scented quaffs to rich reds roiling with gravelly black plum flavors, California's Cabernet can produce it all. Arguably the best, however, come from Napa.

Napa's Star

Cabernet Sauvignon's favorite home is the Napa Valley, a long, thin valley framed by San Pablo Bay to the south and the Mayacamas Mountains to the west. Here, up in the mountains that frame the valley, the sun beats down on vines that barely have any soil to hold on to, while the altitude keeps them cool, especially at night. The result is Cabernet Sauvignon with flavors as intense as its tannins, at once both ripe and hard as nails.

Quick Sip

A few of Napa's cult Cabs:

- Caymus
- Dalle Valle
- Diamond Creek
- Grace Family
- Harlan
- Screaming Eagle

Down on the valley floor, in places like Oakville and Rutherford, Cabernet Sauvignon can be outstanding, too, coddled in sunshine and fed by the valley's unique soils.

To find Napa Cabernet Sauvignon, look for wines labeled "Napa Valley" or with any of the following AVAs, or American Viticultural Areas, the U.S. equivalent of France's appellations:

- Atlas Peak
- Chiles Valley
- Diamond Mountain
- Howell Mountain
- Mount Veeder
- Oakville
- Pope Valley
- Rutherford
- Spring Mountain
- Stags Leap

Napa may be the most famous place in California for great Cabernet, but you'll find good examples in other parts of the state, too.

Beyond Napa

You'll find many good Cabernets labeled simply "California," which means the grapes could have come from anyplace in the state, but there are a few other regions to seek out. For one, try Sonoma, the huge region that sprawls from the Mayacamas to the sea and produces a variety of Cabernet Sauvignon styles. Some of the best come from the rugged, warm regions of …

- Alexander Valley.
- Dry Creek Valley.
- Knights Valley.
- Sonoma Mountain.

Look also to the Santa Cruz Mountains, which grow Cabernets as untamed as the area's forests, and to Paso Robles's sun-warmed, ocean-cooled vineyards for dense, rich variations.

Cabernet Down Under

Cabernet Sauvignon grows all over the Southern Hemisphere, with some of the best examples coming out of Australia. Variations can range from smooth and simple (broad, warm Southeastern Australia) to tannic and earthy with funky flavors (hot, flat Coonawarra with its rust-colored soils), to lean and Bordeaux-like (cool Western Australia.)

Chile and Argentina have also gotten into the act, though they fare better with native grapes Malbec (Chapter 13) and Carmènere (Chapter 9). Still, if you're looking for value, these countries are good places to start.

Blending Prowess

In Bordeaux, vintners normally blend bits of other grapes into their Cabernet wines. It's not surprising, then, that vintners around the world have followed suit. What they blend depends on what they have; for instance, in Italy's Tuscany region, vintners will often blend Cabernet Sauvignon with the native Sangiovese. The resulting wines are often referred to as Super Tuscans, a reference to their pumped-up, powerful flavors and potential for aging.

In many places, however, vintners directly inspired by Bordeaux make what's referred to as a Bordeaux blend, a blend of one or more of the grapes traditional to Bordeaux: Cabernet Sauvignon, Cabernet Franc, Carmènere, Malbec, Merlot, and Petit Verdot. In California, some vintners call these Bordeaux blends Meritage (pronounced like "heritage") wines.

How to find Bordeaux blends from outside of Bordeaux if the label doesn't say Meritage? Often they're the ones with the mysterious name on the label, and not much more, like Camaspelo from Cayuse, or Alluvium from California's Beringer Vineyards. Either that, or they're simply labeled "Estate Red Wine," as is the Bordeaux blend from Washington State's Woodward Canyon.

Quick Sip

Super Cabernet blends from around the world:

- Sassicaia (Tuscany)
- Grosset Gaia (Australia)
- Vega Sicilia Único (Spain)
- Fabre Montmayou Grand Vin (Argentina)
- Skouras Megas Oenos (Greece)
- Château Musar (Lebanon)

Cabernet's Father, Franc

While looking for Cabernet Sauvignon, you may come across Cabernet Franc. Don't pass it over. It, too, can be great. In fact, Cabernet Sauvignon owes its existence to Franc: The grape resulted from a cross between the red grape Cabernet Franc and the white Sauvignon Blanc, according to DNA analysis.

Cab Franc, as it's fondly called by its fans, has similar black currant flavors to Cabernet Sauvignon, but with a lighter texture and more herbal or foresty notes. The most famous versions are grown in France's Loire Valley, where the cool temperatures keep Cabernet Franc frisky and bright, the perfect red wines for slurping with *steak frites* and duck à *l'orange* in Paris cafés.

Cabernet Franc also does well on Long Island, in New York State, as well as in Napa, California, where the sun coaxes out fruitier, plumper flavors.

Quick Sip

Hotbeds for Loire Cab Franc:

- Anjou (ahn-*zhou*): The lightest Cab Franc, for summer days
- Bourgeuil (bore-*goy*): Frisky, black currant-scented beauties
- Chinon (she-*nown*): Dark, chewy Cab Franc
- Saumur (so-*mure*): Light and fruity reds fit for fish

Cab Costs

As with many of the best things in life, Cabernet Sauvignon and its blends can cost an arm, a leg, and a torso, too. The most esteemed wines can go for several hundred dollars a bottle. Wines from well-regarded appellations like Margaux, Pauillac, St-Éstephe, and St-Julien in France and some from California's Napa Valley run from $20 to $100.

What do you get for your money? A regal, long-lived Cabernet Sauvignon—that will often not taste so good if you open it up immediately after purchase. Expensive Cabernets and Cabernet blends are meant to be cellared for a few years (or decades, depending on the year and the winery). If you open them only two or three years after the vintage, the tannins may well be so tough and drying as to be unpleasant. With time, the tannin will loosen its grip.

Off the Vine

When ordering tannic wines like Cabernet Sauvignon, order some protein to go with them. If you have steak, a burger, or some cheese with your tannic red wine, the tannin will bind to the protein in the food instead of to your tongue.

If you want Cabernet Sauvignon or a Bordeaux blend for drinking tonight, look for wines under $30. For Bordeaux in particular, scope out wines labeled simply "Bordeaux" or "Bordeaux Supérior," or search out lesser-known Bordeaux-area appellations like Côtes de Bourg, Côtes de Blaye, Côtes de Castillon, and Premières Côtes de Bordeaux. While they don't have the cachet of the bigger names, they often offer firm, black-fruited Cabernet Sauvignon for a fraction of the price.

Also seek out second-label wines. These are wines made from grapes that are good, but not quite up to snuff for an estate's flagship bottling. Instead of wasting the grapes, many wineries make another wine under a second label and sell it for less. With second-label wines, you get a taste of the winery's style and prowess for a fraction of the price of their regular wine.

Chapter 9

Merlot

In This Chapter

- Why Merlot is loved and hated
- Bordeaux's Right Bank Merlot
- Washington's pride
- Chile's Carmenère

Merlot makes wine that wine snobs hate to love: The grape's wines are always so juicy, plush, plummy, and, well, friendly. That's why Merlot is on every wine list and the Merlot shelf takes up at least 12 feet of every wine store. It's second only to Cabernet Sauvignon in popularity in the United States, and vintners all over the world have adopted it as their own. As with Cabernet, to get to know the grape, it's best to start in Bordeaux.

Bordeaux's Right Bank Hero

Merlot grows nearly everywhere vines grow, but few regions can match France's Right Bank Bordeaux. While Cabernet Sauvignon is the champion in the

Left Bank's gravel soils, Merlot thrives on the right side of the Gironde, where cold clay soils and warmer air allow the grapes to get slowly, evenly ripe.

Just as with the Left Bank's Cabernet-based wines, the Right Bank's Merlot wines are often blended with bits of Cabernet Sauvignon and its relative, Cabernet Franc. Merlot can lack a little structure on its own, so the Cabernet's strong tannin and acidity help to give it more backbone.

The results, for great Right Bank wines, are wines of velvet texture and plush, cushy fruit, with just enough structure to prevent them from being dull but not get in the way of pleasure. Unlike Left Bank wines, which need years of age to show their best, Right Bank Merlots are often pleasurable right away—although good ones can keep well for a decade or two.

> ## Sour Grapes
>
> St-Émilion has a classification scheme different from the rest of Bordeaux, in which the top wines are called Premiers Grands Crus Classés, and the next level is Grands Crus Classés, followed finally by Grand Cru without the "Classé."

Of course, to find Right Bank Merlot, you'll have to look for appellations in the area. The most famous Right Bank appellations are …

- St-Émilion, revered for its sweet, concentrated fruit.
- Pomerol, admired for lush fruit surrounding a firm mineral core.

Before you go running off to the store, know that Good Pomerol and St-Émilion can run $30 to well over $100. To find more affordable Merlot, look to nearby appellations like …

- The Côtes de Bourg, Blaye, Castillon, and Francs.
- Fronsac and Canon-Fronsac.
- Lalande-de-Pomerol.
- Lussac-St-Émilion and Puisseguin-St-Émilion.

Or look to the Languedoc in France's south, where warm temperatures make for fat, juicy Merlot. It may not have the structure and longevity of Right Bank Merlot, but its bodacious flavors are perfect for a party, especially at less than $12.

Merlot, American Style

Merlot grows all over the United States, from Long Island to Texas to Washington State. It's there, in the far northwestern corner of the country, where the grape truly excels—though California's examples offer tough competition.

Washington's Stellar Merlot

When it comes to Merlot, Washington soars past California in quality. It's not that California doesn't have some spectacular Merlot; it's just that the quality isn't as uniformly high. Washington State's Merlot also tends to be more hedonistic, so rich and plush it recalls Black Forest cake, but deeper, richer, and more savory.

The majority of Washington's best Merlot grows in the Columbia Valley, a dry, sunny area on the eastern side of the Cascades. The entire AVA is some 11,000 acres, some of which extends into Oregon. Although many Washington Merlots bear the Columbia Valley AVA, vintners have identified a few areas within the region that grow Merlots of a particular character. These AVAs are as follows:

- **Red Mountain**—Merlot with muscle
- **Walla Walla**—Powerful, plush Merlot
- **Yakima Valley**—Lighter, finer Merlot

Just because a wine sports the name of a large region doesn't mean it's less good than one from a more geographically specific subappellation. Some wineries prefer to have the freedom to blend grapes from different areas, using their different characteristics to make a complex, balanced wine. Other vintners prefer to concentrate on specific areas, to capture that place's taste in the bottle. It's up to you to decide which wines you prefer.

California's Competitors

Merlot seems to lap up the sun, turning its heat directly into juice. That means Merlot can grow in any region of California, for better or worse.

See, the problem is, when Merlot ripens too quickly, or when it's made with an eye toward quantity, not quality, the result can be Merlot that tastes more like melted jam fermented in a bell pepper. In other words, it can be pretty disgusting.

When California Merlot is good, though, it can be some of the most hedonistic juice around, full of plush, plummy flavor often boosted by sweet vanilla notes from time spent in oak barrels. To find this sort of Merlot, stay out of the hot Central Valley and look instead to the challenging terrain of the Napa Valley, or to Sonoma Valley's sunny but cooler spots. Expect, however, to pay for the pleasure: Reliably good California Merlot starts at $15 and rises rapidly from there.

Mountain Merlot

Merlot has one other stronghold: in Europe, on either side of the Alps. In Switzerland, the cool temperatures make for light, sharp Merlot labeled Merlot del Ticino, the name of the canton where the grape thrives. These Merlots work best when they are sipped with a beef fondue or other rich food that appreciates their high acidity. Over the Alps in Italy, Merlot ripens just enough in the coolness of Veneto and Friuli to make some mouthwatering pours. These tend to be light and acidic, with re-freshing red cherry and plum flavors. They are easy to find because they'll always carry the name of the grape on the label.

Merlot grows farther south, too, most notably in Tuscany, where it's typically blended with Cabernet Sauvignon and/or the native Sangiovese to make a Super Tuscan blend. The few 100-percent Merlot wines available tend to be some of the most hedo-nistic pours around, as rich and beautiful as the region is easy on the eyes. Unfortunately, most are priced well above $20.

Southern Styles

The Southern Hemisphere is chock full of Merlot, most successfully, perhaps, in Australia, which turns out gallons of it in the "Aussie good drink" style, meaning affordable and easy to drink.

Chile had been doing a knockout business in Merlot until it discovered that much of what it had been calling Merlot was actually another grape called Carmenère. No matter: whether it's Merlot or Carmenère disguised as Merlot, it makes a plummy, rich red in Chile that sells for a song—great ver-sions can be had for $10.

Carmenère, Merlot's Long-Lost Friend

Over the past few years, more Chilean wineries have been labeling wines Carmenère. This grape, which they used to confuse with Merlot, is an old variety native to Bordeaux but almost extinct there today. In Chile, however, Carmenère thrives, producing blackberry-juicy wines suffused with a foresty scent, like the Andes on a rainy day. For an armchair trip to Chile, it's worth every penny of the $10 to $20.

Quick Sip _____

Carmenère is sometimes called Grande Vidure.

Buying Merlot

Merlot is one grape variety for which it really pays not to skimp. It's possible to find good $10-and-under versions, but it isn't easy, and bad Merlot is really terrible.

Quick Sip _____

Good-value Merlot:
- Concha y Toro Casillero del Diablo, Chile
- J. Lohr, Paso Robles
- Lindemans, South Australia
- Powers, Columbia Valley
- Sagelands, Columbia Valley

So when you're on a budget, look to budget wine strongholds like Languedoc, France; Chile; and Southeastern Australia: All three areas put out gallons of gulpable Merlot, the sort of wines that go well with burgers and barbecues.

Look also for Chile's Carmenère, which tends to pack more complexity and structure for the price than Merlot can. Good examples start at $10.

For the rest of the world, I'm sorry to say, you're best off paying at least $15, and the wines should only get better as you move up in price. No wonder it's a grape wine lovers hate to love.

10

Pinot Noir

In This Chapter

- Why the fuss?
- Parsing Burgundy's Pinot patchwork
- Oregon's great Pinots
- Pinot prices

There's a book about Pinot Noir famously titled *The Heartbreak Grape* by Marq de Villiers. In those three words, De Villiers captured the essence of Pinot Noir: heartbreakingly beautiful when done well, and heartbreakingly frustrating because it's so difficult to do well.

Pinot: Pain and Pleasure

Pinot Noir is a thin-skinned grape: It doesn't like to be too warm or too cold, too wet or too dry. When it is, the grape refuses to ripen in any way that would produce pleasurable wines. When Pinot is bad, it's really bad.

But when Pinot Noir is good, it's the stuff of dreams. Though it may not look so impressive in the glass, its color light and flat, like pale velvet more than silk, its flavors pack more soul than most grapes do fruit. To taste the reasons Pinot Noir has become revered, it's best to once again head to France, where the grape established its reputation, but it's worth checking out what it does in other parts of the world, especially Oregon, New Zealand, and parts of Australia.

Burgundian Dreams

Burgundy's gray skies and cool temperatures might seem drab to lots of people, but it's heaven for Pinot Noir. Nice and cool, Pinot Noir can take its time ripening, in which time it packs on spice and minerals the way other grapes pack on juicy fruit.

The result is an array of Pinot Noirs that taste very particularly of a place; in other words, they have terroir. The Burgundians find Pinot Noir's sense of terroir so strong that they don't label the wines by grape, but by place, or appellation (AOC).

Quick Sip

Burgundy is complicated, but this part is easy: If it's red, you can pretty much bet that it's made from Pinot Noir.

Burgundy has hundreds of appellations, each defined by the geographical and climatic differences that affect the final flavor of the Pinot. It sounds excessive, but beware: Those who fall for Pinot become obsessed by these sorts of details.

Lay of the Land

Getting to know red Burgundy requires getting to know a little about the lay of the land—especially since the wines aren't labeled by grape, but by place. The most basic red Burgundies are labeled simply *Bourgogne Rouge* (bore-*gon* rooj, French for red Burgundy), which means the grapes that went into them could have come from anywhere within the entire region. Most are light and supple, $10 to $20 reds that make great by-the-glass pours.

If the grapes are pulled from only one village, the wine most likely won't say "Bourgogne." It will be labeled only with the name of the village. The buyer is expected to know that it's in Burgundy. The following are the names of Pinot Noir villages in Burgundy, listed from north to south as they fall geographically:

- Marsannay
- Fixin
- Gevrey-Chambertin
- Morey-St-Denis
- Chambolle-Musigny
- Vougeot
- Vosne-Romanée

- Flagey-échezeaux
- Nuits-St-George
- Ladoix
- Pernand-Vergelesses
- Aloxe-Corton
- Chorey-lès-Beaune
- Savigny-lès-Beaune
- Beaune
- Pommard
- Volnay
- Ladoix-Serrigny
- Auxey-Duresses
- Monthélie
- St-Romain
- St-Aubin
- Mercurey
- Givry
- Rully (mostly white wines, but some good red bargains)

You could memorize this list, but there are probably better things to do with your time. What's more important to know is that there are even more exacting classifications to these AOCs.

Grand Trumps Premier

True perfectionists, the Burgundians have singled out 561 Burgundian vineyards as Premier Cru ("first growth") and another 30 as the even more respected Grand Cru ("great growth").

Quick Sip

Grand Grands:

- Domaine Roumier Bonnes-Mares
- Joseph Drouhin Charmes-Chambertin
- Mongeard-Mugneret Echézeaux
- Nicolas Potel Chambertin
- Tollot-Beaut Corton-Bressandes

Sometimes, however, Burgundians don't bother noting Premier or Grand Cru on the label; they just offer the name of the vineyard. The buyer is expected to know how the vineyard ranks. But don't worry: If you don't know, the steep prices (generally $60 and up) make Grand Cru bottlings stand out.

France's Other Pinot Haven

Burgundy isn't the only place in France to find Pinot Noir. The picky grape also grows in the central Loire Valley, where the cool, continental climate leads to some of the lightest Pinot Noir around.

Once again, the wines won't say "Pinot Noir" on the label. Instead, look for red wines from …

- Sancerre.
- Menetou-Salon.

Loire Pinot Noirs are the sorts of wines often found in casual Parisian bistros poured by the carafe. They might not have the same sort of grace and finesse as those in Burgundy, but they are right at home with a thin hanger steak and a pile of fries.

Oregon's Excellent Options

Outside of Burgundy, France, there's no place that does Pinot Noir as consistently well as Oregon. Most of it grows in the Willamette (pronounced will-*am*-et) Valley, which sits up in the northwest corner of the state.

Framed in by mountains on three sides and the Columbia River, the 100-mile valley stays cool enough for the cool-loving grape, yet it's a little sunnier and warmer than Burgundy. The resulting wines are a bit deeper in color and, likewise, in fruit flavor, with a little less funk than classic Burgundy. Nonetheless, they retain the spicy, earthy fragrance that sets Pinot Noir apart from any other grape's wines, and they remain light enough to pair well with the region's meaty salmon.

Farther south, the warmer Umpqua Valley puts out meatier Pinot Noir, the sort for roast chicken or duck. Or course, you could keep on going on into California ….

California Coming Up

California's relentless sun and good weather are exactly what sent winemakers into the cooler, rainier reaches of Oregon to grow Pinot Noir, but some California vintners have persevered to good effect. The state's best Pinot Noir grows in its coolest regions, such as these:

- Sonoma Coast
- Russian River Valley (including Green Valley and Chalk Hill)
- Carneros
- Santa Barbara (including Santa Ynez and Santa Maria Valleys)

Few parts of these American Viticultural Areas (AVAs) ever get really cold, so, in fact, Pinot Noir can get very ripe—it just does it slowly. The resulting wines often have very concentrated Pinot Noir fruit flavors, yet they remain fragrant and light on the tongue, due to their ability to hold on to their lively acidity.

Far-Flung Pinot Outposts

Great Pinot Noir is so beguiling that there's probably not a place on Earth where someone hasn't tried growing it. There are a handful of decent examples coming out of places as disparate as Chile and Germany (where they call it Spätburgunder, worth buying just for an opportunity to say "*schpate*-bur-*gun*-der.")

> **Off the Vine**
>
> In Italy, Pinot Noir is called Pinot Nero (*peen*-o *nair*-o); in German-speaking countries, it's called Spätburgunder (*schpate*-bur-*gun*-der).

It might be easier, though, to stick with Pinot Noir. Here are some highlights of the variety around the world.

New Zealand

One place that's done pretty well with Pinot is New Zealand, especially in the following regions:

- Wairarapa
- Martinborough
- Canterbury
- Central Otago

These cool areas produce some of the most intense Pinot Noir around, often with deep color and rich, velvety textures. It's Pinot Noir for winter nights and for people who find Burgundian examples too light.

Australia's Options

Over in Australia, a few vintners have had success with the variety in places such as these:

- Tasmania
- Victoria (including Yarra Valley, Geelong, Mornington Peninsula)
- Adelaide Hills
- Eden Valley

Tasmania is so cold that the Pinot Noir often goes into Champagne-styled sparkling wines; the still versions are typically as light and frisky as they come. The other three areas are warmer and have richer results, often accenting fruit over earth.

New York's Pinot Possibilities

Perhaps the most Burgundian examples outside of Burgundy are coming out of New York State—although, truth be told, there aren't many. However, in the state's chilly Finger Lakes, which have proven to be ideal for cold-loving Riesling, Pinot Noir is staking a place for itself with spicy, mineral-tinged, dried cherry-flavored beauties, at once ethereal and substantial.

What Price Pinot

It's heartbreaking, but to really experience good Pinot Noir, it'll cost you. The grape is simply difficult to grow and to make, and inspired examples don't come cheap.

But don't give up. The really pricey stuff isn't meant for everyday drinking anyway. If you can afford a Grand Cru Burgundy or a $50 Pinot from anywhere else, by all means, buy it, but don't drink it right away. Great Burgundy gets better with time, and it doesn't begin to show its full glory for 5, 10, or 15 years.

While you're waiting for it to come around, or, when you don't have time to wait, look to the $10 to $30 price range. These wines tend to be delicious upon opening (though many will age well, too). And they don't break the bank.

And there are a few bargains here and there that make Pinot Noir an option for everyday drinking. Here are a few from around the world:

- **Australia**—Lindemans Bin 99
- **Burgundy**—Joseph Drouhin La Fôret Bourgogne
- **California**—Navarro Mendocino
- **Chile**—Cono Sur
- **New York**—Fox Run
- **New Zealand**—Twin Islands
- **Oregon**—Erath

That's not many, but keep looking. Great, affordable Pinot Noir is worth the search.

Syrah

In This Chapter

- Syrah with a French accent
- The Aussie's Shiraz
- America's sexiest grape?
- Petite Sirah

Whether it's called Syrah or Shiraz, this red grape makes some of the most sultry, spicy, exotic reds on the market. More giving than Cabernet Sauvignon, more structured than most Merlot, and denser than Pinot Noir, Syrah is a grape that fills a need—a need for more different types of deliciousness in our lives. Lucky us: Syrah thrives in France, Australia, California, and Washington State.

Syrah with a French Accent

Syrah (seer-*ah*) tends to be the name most commonly heard for this grape, and rightly so, many would claim, because the French name points to the grape's most famous home: the Rhône Valley, France.

The Rhône Valley is a long one, starting in the decidedly chilly, continental climate of Lyon and winding down to the warm, Mediterranean air around Avignon. Because the differences from one end to the other are so great, it's often talked about as two regions: the Northern and the Southern Rhône.

Northern Delights

The Northern Rhône is all about extremes: extremely steep riverbanks, extremely rich food, and cold winters followed by hot summers. It's beautiful, but not an easy life for a grapevine, and there's only two that hack it: Viognier (a white wine discussed in Chapter 13) and Syrah.

Remember, though, that we're talking about France, where they don't label wines by grapes. Instead, Rhône Syrah will sport the name of an appellation, which will be one of the following:

- Côte-Rôtie
- Hermitage
- St-Joseph
- Crozes-Hermitage

Côte-Rôtie and Hermitage are the most intense wines of the four appellations because their steep angles and rocky, poor soil give Syrah a tough challenge. The vines' effort is borne out in their wines' concentrated, gripping flavors, dense with almost roasted fruit and firm, earthy minerality.

Because of that intensity, both Hermitage and Côte-Rôtie wines are better drunk after some 10 years of age, during which they can let up their tannic grip and develop more of the earthy, spicy flavors that make them so sexy.

> ### Off the Vine
>
> When vintners talk about blending grapes, they are usually referring to grapes of the same color. But in the Northern Rhône, vintners are allowed to add a dash of the white grape Viognier to Syrah's black flavors, which lends the wine a delicate floral note.

While you're waiting for Hermitage and Côte-Rôtie wines to reach their peak, seek out Syrah from nearby St-Joseph and Crozes-Hermitage. Both appellations lie on gentler land and give likewise gentler wines. They are typically a whole lot cheaper, too: Good ones tend to run about $10 to $20, as opposed to the $50-and-up bottles from the fancier appellations.

Southern Syrah

Head south from Hermitage, and the slopes flatten out as the river valley widens. Bright sun and hillsides of purple lavender are reminders that Provence isn't far away. This area is called the Rhône, but the climate is decidedly Mediterranean.

There's another element that sets the Southern Rhône apart from the northern section: Syrah is no longer the only red grape. Joining it are Grenache, Mourvèdre, Cinsault, and a host of other lesser-known varieties. Typically, southern Rhône reds are made from a combination of these varieties, though Syrah is often the dominant grape. For a taste of these Southern Rhône blends, look to these places:

- **Gigondas**—Gravelly, tannic Syrah
- **Vacquerays**—Very similar to Gigondas
- **Châteauneuf-du-Pape**—Spicy, sophisticated Southern Rhônes, made complex by blending up to 13 different grape varieties
- **Lirac**—Lyrical Syrah, smooth and easy
- **Rasteau**—Cherry lollipop fun

There's more Syrah available if you keep going south, into the sprawling Languedoc-Roussillon. In this warm region that hugs the Mediterranean, some pockets produce strong, structured Syrah, but the overwhelming majority of wines are juicy $8 buys labeled by the grape variety.

The rest of the best Syrah in the world are labeled by grape variety, too—as in Australia.

Australia

The Aussies call Syrah Shiraz (sheer-*azzz*), after the capitol of the grape variety's supposed birthplace, Persia. The Aussies produce styles ranging from $8 gulpables grown on the warm flatlands of southeastern Australia, to lean, chewy, sophisticated pours from cooler reaches. Nonetheless, it's often easy to tell Australian Shiraz apart from French Syrah because of its ebullient fruitiness and clean, bright flavors. Often vintners will age Shiraz in American oak, which adds lush notes of vanilla and sometimes coconut to the wine's already sweet cherry-plum notes.

To have an idea of what you're getting when you buy an Aussie Shiraz, look at the appellation. The following are the big ones, with notes on the style of Shiraz you can expect from each:

- **Barossa**—Substantial Shiraz, fat with rich, dense, sweet fruit flavors
- **Hunter Valley**—Funky, earthy Shiraz
- **McLaren Vale**—Almost as big as Barossa Shiraz
- **Southeastern Australia**—Juicy, simple $5-to-$12 reds
- **Victoria**—Muscular, dense Shiraz
- **Western Australia**—Lean, Northern Rhône–like Shiraz

If you forget what sort of Syrah comes from which region, price often offers a good tip-off to the style in the bottle. Juicy, easy Shiraz sells for equally easy prices, from $2.99 up to about $12.

> **Off the Vine**
>
> Some Australian Shiraz smells a bit like a peppermint patty, with a distinctly minty note sandwiched between its chocolaty fruit. Some people think it's the nature of the grapes in certain areas; others point to the numerous eucalyptus trees as the source.

Above $12 to about $25 are the Shiraz to bring to dinner at a friend's house: solid, ready to drink, with plenty of fruit kept fresh and firm by spicy acidity and pleasantly gritty tannin.

Above $25, you're into the blockbusters, the wines that pack in enough fruit, tannin, and acidity for a side of beef—or to last them a decade in the wine cellar. As the price suggests, these are special-occasion wines, and those occasions had better feature some serious protein.

California's Sexy Syrah

Syrah came late to American vintner's attention, mainly because the area's winemakers were first more inspired to imitate the classic wines of Bordeaux and Burgundy. But in the 1980s, a group of vintners banded together to promote Syrah as a better fit for California's warm climate. The Rhône Rangers, as they were called, were scoffed at in the early days, but with the array of smoky, chocolaty, cherry-filled, spice-scented beauties the state puts out today, it's clear the Rhône Rangers were on the right track.

Santa Barbara Syrah

Santa Barbara has made a name for itself in Syrah. The large region, only about two hours up the coast from Los Angeles, has a range of climates within it, each of which produces a slightly different style of Syrah. In general, you can expect Santa Barbara Syrah to be dense yet juicy, with black fruit and even black-olive flavors and firm tannin, but it's worth looking to these subappellations within Santa Barbara County for different styles:

- Santa Ynez Valley's cool yet sunny weather allows the grapes to ripen slowly over a long season, making for Syrah with lots of spice and earth tones surrounding a core of sweet red-cherry flavor.

- Santa Maria Valley is even cooler that Santa Ynez, so its Syrahs are even leaner, with lots of spice and mineral tones, more Northern Rhône in style than Southern.

California's Other Pockets

Santa Barbara's success with Syrah has spurred on vintners in other regions to try their hands at it. It seems to do pretty well almost everywhere, just producing different styles depending on the climate. For example, Napa's Syrah, which basks in the sun in a protected valley, tends to be dense and chunky with sweet fruit. Sonoma's are spicier; those from cool regions such as Russian River Valley can be downright peppery. Head into even chillier realms, such as Mendocino, and the Syrah is light and frisky, with high acidity that makes its red-cherry flavors dance.

Quick Sip

If a California wine calls itself Shiraz, you can bet it's been made with the Australian style in mind: rich, ripe, and sweetened by the vanilla tones of American oak.

Regardless where it comes from, you can get a good idea of what sort of Syrah is in the bottle by the price. Simple, light Wednesday-night-roast-chicken-breast-dinner wines run $6 to $12; step up to $15 or $20, and there should be plenty enough concentrated flavor for a steak.

At more than $20, a Syrah should offer the same things a French Syrah does: elegance, with deep, rich flavors made mesmerizing by spice and mineral notes—except, of course, with a bright, sunny core of California fruitiness.

Petite Sirah

No, it's not spelled wrong, and it's not just a little, slimmed-down version of Syrah: Although it may be related, Petite Sirah is a different grape variety. Like Syrah, it's an old French grape, but it's almost impossible to find any in France these days. Lucky for us wine lovers, the variety loves the sun and warmth of California and puts out deep, dark black wines, dense with black-plum flavors backed in tannins. They are terrific choices for cold nights and hearty stews.

Washington's Hedonistic Syrah

There's one last pocket of super Syrah in the States: Washington State's sun-soaked Columbia Valley. As with Washington's Merlot (see Chapter 9), the sun seems to turbo-charge the vines, allowing them to produce some of the sexiest Syrah around, saturated with soft, ripe, even chocolaty fruit flavor, yet firm with acidity and tannin. You'll pay for the best, though: good deals are hard to find for less than $18, and wines can easily command $30 or more, especially for single-vineyard examples.

Chapter 12

Zinfandel

In This Chapter

- The pink stuff
- The real, red stuff
- The truth about "old vines"
- The Italian connection

California makes a lot of great wine, but no wine is as close to Californian's hearts as Zinfandel. Like all the major wine grapes covered in this book, Zinfandel came from Europe, but California is the only place on the planet that makes Zinfandel with such aplomb. Whether light and jazzy or black as night, Zinfandels are some of the most delicious wines made in this country.

Not So Proudly Pink

Many people know Zinfandel as a pink wine called White Zinfandel, though it's the grape's least proud form. Zinfandel is a grape so deeply colored it looks black, and, when made like most red wines (that is, pressed and the juice left to mull with its skins), it can make some of the darkest wines on the market.

Back in the 1960s, when white wine was all the rage, American's didn't go for red Zinfandel. But California had a lot of acres of Zinfandel—it's a good, sturdy vine that can grow almost anywhere, and it can produce lots of juice. Something had to be done or lots of Zinfandel would go to waste.

What happened nearly changed the definition of the grape variety. In 1972, Bob Trinchero at Sutter Home Winery in Napa, California, took some Zinfandel grapes and drew off the *free-run* juice— that is, the juice that seeps out of the grapes naturally, simply from the weight of the grapes themselves. Because free-run juice hasn't spent much time in contact with the grape skins, the juice doesn't pick up much color (remember, the color pigments of a grape are in the skin, not the juice).

Winespeak

Free-run juice is the juice that seeps out of the grapes from the weight of the grapes themselves, with no added pressure.

Trinchero took the resulting pink juice and bottled it. By 1987, Sutter Home "White Zinfandel" was the most popular wine in the United States. By then, it was no longer being made from just free-run juice, and the style of the wine had become sweeter.

Now that Americans have rediscovered the joy of red wines, White Zinfandel is often made fun of for being pink and slightly sweet. Some of it is truly bad, tasting like candy more than any real fruit. But good versions—like Deloach and Wente—shouldn't be condemned. With slightly sweet watermelon and light strawberry flavors, a hint of spice, and low alcohol (typically around 11 percent, unlike red versions that can soar to 16 percent), good white Zinfandel can make a good companion to spicy take-out Chinese or just a simple easy summer brunch pour—especially when you consider the $5-to-$12 prices.

At the same time, White Zinfandel isn't the type of wine that gathers rabid fans. That sort of devotion requires a wine that's spicy, feisty, soulful, and even a little mysterious—like Zinfandel, the red stuff.

Rockin' Red Zinfandel

It's red and juicy, but Zinfandel isn't like any other grape. There's something about it—a certain wildness that sets it apart from buttoned-down Cabernet Sauvignon; a profound darkness that differentiates it from the plump, easy pleasure of Merlot; an untamed spiciness that stands apart from the silky spice of Syrah—it's hard to describe. You'll just have to taste some for yourself.

Slim and Sassy

Zin is commonly thought of as a big, bodaciously built wine, but they aren't all that way. In cooler regions, the grape ripens slowly, taking on ripe plum fruit flavors while retaining its bright, spicy acidity. The result is a red that's slim but still strong, with the sort of spice, acid, and tannin that can take on a ribeye as well as treat a roast chicken with care.

To find slim, sassy Zinfandel, look to …

- Mendocino.
- Russian River Valley.

Mendocino Zins are the lighter of the two; Russian River Valley versions can skate into the strong and elegant category, up next.

Strong Yet Elegant

Move to a slightly warmer region, and you'll find slightly richer Zinfandel. Sonoma is a particular stronghold for the variety; it's been planted here since the first Italian immigrants arrived in the area, and there's now more of it here than anyplace else in California. For particular standouts, look to these:

- **Dry Creek Valley**—Home base for some of Zinfandel's most famous names, including Dashe, Quivira, Ridge (Lytton Springs), Rafanelli, Rancho Zabaco, and Ravenswood (Teldeschi Vineyard). These tend to be a step darker and spicier than those from nearby Russian River Valley.
- **Alexander Valley**—Chocolate-dense Zin with bright cherry centers, such as those Rosenblum and Seghesio show.

Quick Sip

Great Zinfandel values:

- Cline California Zinfandel
- Ravenswood Vintners Blend
- Rosenblum Vintner's Cuvée
- Sutter Home
- Wild Horse Paso Robles

A side note: When looking for California Zin, you'll often come across bottles that say "old vines" on the label. Is it important? Maybe. The older vines get, the fewer grapes they produce; the fewer grapes per vine, the more intense the flavor is in the grapes. "Old vines" is a way of suggesting that the wine has particularly deep, intense flavors, and often it does. But here's the catch: There is no legal definition of "old." Those advertised "old vines" could be 15 or 100 years old, depending on who's doing the defining. The only thing you can do is taste the wine and decide whether you think it's worth the money.

Big and Brooding

This is the style of red wines that Zinfandel built its name on: massive, dense, sweet, and spicy. There are many from which to choose; here are some highlights from the state:

- **Lodi**—A mother lode of Zin—flat and warm, yet cooled by ocean breezes that let the grapes get prodigiously ripe.

- **Sierra Foothills,** including Amador, El Dorado, Fiddletown, and Shenandoah—Black plums and black pepper make an intense combination.

- **Paso Robles**—Hot days and cold nights make for plump, super-fruity, yet structured Zin.

- **Napa**—Dark, muscled Zinfandel, especially when grown up close to the sun in the rough, cool peaks of Howell Mountain, Diamond Mountain, or Mt. Veeder.

Quick Sip

Extreme Zinfandel:

- Chateau Potelle VGS
- d-Cubed
- Girard
- Justin
- Ridge Lytton Springs
- Rosenblum Monte Rosso
- Storybook Mountain Mayacamas Range

These aren't the only areas of California that make good Zinfandel; even the generically labeled Zinfandels that are made from grapes grown in places more suited to artichokes can be pretty darn tasty for the price. It's this sort of versatility that makes it appealing to vintners around the world.

Zinfandel Abroad

Not surprisingly, Zinfandel has made its way across the border into Mexico, where Chateau Camou makes a spicy approximation. The variety has also grabbed the attention of the Australians, who are hoping it will thrive in their sunny, warm spots, too; even a few Frenchmen are experimenting with plantings.

But before any of these countries got into Zin, Southern Italy was way ahead of them. The Italians have been growing a grape called Primitivo for ages, and DNA studies show the grape to be genetically identical to Zinfandel, though the flavors aren't quite the same.

Quick Sip

Some of Italy's best Primitivos come from the region Primitivo di Manduria. Check out A-Mano, Apollonio, and Terrale for examples. A bonus: Most examples run about $10.

To taste for yourself, look to Apulia. There in the heel of Italy's boot, you'll find the jammy purple wines that have quenched the thirst of Apulians long before we came to know the grape as Zinfandel.

Blends, Bubbles, and Beyond

Now you're familiar with all the grapes you're most likely to see on a wine label. That's *a lot* of wine. But it's not everything; in fact, some of the most exciting, delicious wines come from grapes that rarely leave the confines of their country. And what would life be without sweet wines or, heaven forbid, bubbles? They are all here in Part 4.

Chapter 13

The Best of the Rest

In This Chapter

- Making obscure grapes familiar
- Exploring little-known wine regions
- Finding great values where others don't look

There are more grapes in the world than we could possibly cover in this tiny book, and there are even more wines that result from blending different grapes. However, there are some wines you really shouldn't miss. The grape names may be unfamiliar, and the places foreign, but those challenges are worth overcoming for the pleasure the wines give. Another bonus: Lesser-known wines often sell for less. Bargain hunters, take note!

Wonderful Whites

No country can live on red wine alone; even those places where red's the rage, vintners devotedly make white wines for those hot days, for seafood, for the times when red just doesn't fit the bill. To make sense of the wealth of choices, it's best to build on what you already know, which are the major varieties. Pick out your favorites, and explore the many options.

Chardonnay-Rich, but Different

Chardonnay's greatest feat is its ability to hold so much luscious flavor, but it's not the only white wine with such guts. Try these whites on for size:

- **Chenin Blanc** makes the rich, waxy wines of the Loire Valley, particularly in Anjou, Saumur, Savennières, and Vouvray. The best last for years, turning caramel-rich and nutty. They aren't cheap, at $15 to $100.

- **Marsanne** and **Roussanne** call France's Rhône Valley home, where together they make broad, almond-scented whites. In California and Australia, they are often vinified separately, allowing Marsanne to show off its waxy marzipan flavors and Roussanne its deeply golden, honeyed stone fruit notes.

- **Vermentino** gets fat and happy in the warmth of the Mediterranean, particularly in Sicily and Sardinia. Most run about $10, a bargain for the mouthful of pineapple flavor in each sip.

- **Viognier** gives Chardonnay a run for its money in terms of richness. At home in Condrieu, in France's Rhône Valley, its wine offers prodigious amounts of honeyed, peachy flavors; in sunny California, it packs on the peach, pineapple, and vanilla notes. All stand out for their delicate florality, too.

Scented as Sauvignon, with a Twist

Sauvignon Blanc's strength is its bright, snazzy scent and summery fee—but it's not the only grape with those qualities. Try these varieties, too:

- **Gewürztraminer** is named for its flavor: *Gewürz* means "spice." With rose and spice scents on its lycheelike flavors, it can bring an exotic edge to the most mundane dish. It excels in Alsace, though California makes some good ones.

- **Moskofilero** means "friend of Muscat" in Greece, where it grows, and you'll understand why when you taste it and read about the next grape on this list. Its light, flowery flavors are extremely refreshing on a hot day. Spiropoulos and Tselepos make the best examples.

- **Muscat** grows all over the world, and it makes everything from light, dry wines to honey-sweet elixirs. No matter how dry or sweet, all Muscat offers pretty green-grape flavors and floral notes. Try French versions to start.

- **Torrontés** grows in Argentina, where its green, floral flavors lighten up this red-heavy country. Try Susana Balbo's for the grape at its best.

Racy Like Riesling

Riesling stands out for its undefeatable acidity, as well as for its ability to seemingly suck up the flavor of the soil that nourishes it. No grape can do both as well as Riesling, but there are a few that come close:

- **Assyrtiko** makes wines so mineral-heavy they taste like stones more than fruit. (That's a good thing, in the mouth of a terroirist.) And it never lets up its acidity, even though it grows on the hot Greek island of Santorini. The best are labeled simply Santorini; try Boutari Kallisti, Gaia, and Sigalas.

- **Falanghina** makes smoky, mineral wines brightened with lemony acidity. Italy's Campania is its stronghold, especially under the Falerno di Massica DOC.

- **Melon** never shows up on a wine label, but it's the grape responsible for the light, crisp, mineral-tinged whites of Muscadet, France.

- **Scheurebe** (*shoy*-reb-uh) is like Riesling on acid, with similar crisp citrus flavors, but here layered with apricot or even pineapple notes, plus some green herbs. It grows almost exclusively in Pfalz, Germany, where wines are labeled by grape.

- **Tocai Friulano** combines juicy pear flavors, citruslike acidity, and floral notes tinged with nutty, spicy minerality. Find it in Friuli, Italy.

Pinot Grigio–Like Pleasures

Pinot Gris can either be done Italian style, light and fresh, or Alsace style, rich and unctuous. Either way, the wines from this grape make excellent backdrops for fish, vegetables, and white meats. These other grapes that could fill in for Pinot Gris are:

- **Albariño/Alvarinho** is the Spanish/ Portuguese answer to Pinot Grigio, but with more guts. Spanish versions (labeled by variety) tend to be waxy and broad, like Pinot Gris; Portuguese versions come labeled Vinho Verde and are some of the lightest, most refreshing white wines on Earth.

- **Arneis** grows in far northwest Italy, where cool temperatures keep its waxy almond flavor tasting fresh.

Quick Sip

A good way to find good wine values is to look where most other people don't—such as in any of the varieties in this chapter.

- **Fiano di Avellino** grows in Campania, Italy, where its delicate, honey-scented wines provide refreshment on warm days.

- **Greco di Tufo** seems designed with seafood in mind because it's so crisp and simple. Italy's Campania is its home.

- **Ribolla Gialla** makes satin-textured wines with restrained almond notes in Friuli as well as Slovenia.

- **Trebbiano** is the grape behind Italy's simple pleasures Frascati, Galestro, Orvieto, and Est! Est!! Est!!! di Montefiascone. Don't think too hard; just drink.

- **Verdicchio** grows in Le Marche, Italy, where its simple, nutty flavors provide refreshment to serve with seafood.

If you've read this far, your world of wine is immense, yet this is only a taste of the wide world of white wines available. Be adventurous; when you see a white wine you don't know on a by-the-glass wine list, order it. It may become a favorite.

Now on to the reds ....

Reds Not to Be Missed

There's enough variety within the Big Five red wine varieties to last any wine lover a lifetime, but he'd also be missing out. What about southern Italy's sultry, smoky reds? Or its truffled pleasures in the north? How about Argentina's voluptuous Malbec? You'll read about all of them and more in this section.

Cabernet Sauvignon–Like Sips

Tannin, acid, and firm black-fruit flavors make Cabernet Sauvignon one of the most authoritative wines in the world. A few others can match it in temperament and add some qualities of their own:

- **Cot** is the tannic grape behind the "black wines" of Cahors, in southwest France. These wines, labeled Cahors, surpass Cabernet in earthy, gritty tannins and blackness of fruit, and they are terrific with duck and goose, local specialties. To see the smooth side of Cot, see Malbec (a synonym), under "Merlot's Fruity Pleasures," in the next section of this chapter.

- **Baga** has a reputation for making punishingly tannic black wines in its homeland of Bairrada in Portugal, but vintners like Luis Pato are proving that, with care, it can make wines as firm and elegant as great Cabernets, yet with a wonderfully earthy Portuguese slant.

- **Pinotage** is South Africa's favorite red. It's tannic and earthy, like Cabernet, but often packs on lots more blackberry fruit.

- **Refosco** grows in the chill of Friuli in northern Italy, where it develops black-fruit flavors with herbal highlights, lean like cool-climate Cabernet but Italianate. Dorigo, Jermann, Livon, and Ronchi di Manzano make some of the best.

- **Tannat** sounds like *tannic*, which it is, especially in Uruguay. In its French home of Madiran in southwest France, it makes burly, black reds that appreciate beef stews and game.

- **Touriga Nacional** is the Cabernet Sauvignon of Portugal, providing backbone for many blends and sometimes starring as a lean, intense, blackberried wine with herbal scents. Sometimes the grape will appear on the label; otherwise, try wines from Dão and Douro.

Merlot's Fruity Pleasures

Merlot's plush, giving fruit is its primary attraction, but other grapes are just as giving. Try these, for instance.

- **Barbera** produces supple, round reds filled with berry flavors all over Italy. The best, however, come from Piedmont, where they are labeled by grape variety. The simplest start at $10; more intense versions run $25 and up.

- **Dolcetto** means "little sweet one" in Italian, which succinctly sums up its easy red cherry flavors. Look for it in Italy's Piedmont region, labeled by grape.

Quick Sip

When you're not sure what a wine is going to taste like, try to imagine the climate of the place in which it was grown. Often the warmer the place, the fruitier and softer the wine—as you can tell from reading about some of the reds in this section.

- **Garnacha,** a.k.a. Grenache in France, makes candy-colored reds with gobs of sweet cherry flavor in Priorat, Spain, as well as Australia, Southern France, and Sardinia, where it's called Cannonau.

- **Montepulciano** makes Merlot-soft and juicy wines in Abruzzo, Italy, where you'll find it labeled Montepulciano d'Abruzzo and it'll cost all of $10.

- **Zweigelt** makes juicy, jammy, blackberry-rich reds in the warmer southern regions of Austria.

Pinot Noir's Earthiness

Pinot's pride is its ethereal flavor, as light as its color yet hard to forget. Its flavors focus more on earth and minerals than on fruit, as do these grapes:

- **Gamay** grows not far from Burgundy, Pinot Noir's home, in Beaujolais. Beaujolais rarely, if ever, gains the complexity of good Pinot Noir, but its translucent, cherry-juicy flavors and brisk acidity make a good stand-in for affordable versions, especially at the under-$25 prices.

- **Nebbiolo** is the grape responsible for the tannic, long-lived reds of Barolo and Barbaresco in northern Italy. They are far brawnier than any Pinot Noir, but, with age, they also offer ethereal, sensuous scents of spice and truffles.

- **Sangiovese** has high acidity that makes all its wines feel frisky even when they carry lots of flavor. You're probably familiar with the grape already: It's the grape in Chianti from Tuscany, Italy.

- **Tempranillo** is tempting in Rioja, where it reflects the warm earth in its spicy cherry-blackberry flavors. In Ribera del Duero, Tempranillo is called Tinto Fino and makes plumper, fruitier wines.

- **Xinomavro** means "sour-black" in Greek, which hints at its high acidity and black color. Its wines have so much acidity they can feel nearly weightless, while at the same time their spicy, truffle-scented, earthy, tannic fruit lodge in the memory. Look for wines labeled Naoussa, the region in which it excels, and give them a few years before opening.

Syrah's Sultriness

Syrah's sultry spice and black fruit make it irresistible to many. For similar experiences, look to these grapes:

- **Aglianico** produces some of southern Italy's best reds: smoky, spicy, and earthy. Look particularly for wines labeled Aglianico del Vulture (from Basilicata) and Aglianico del Taburno or Taurasi (Campania).

- **Carignan** has spice, tannin, earth, and black fruit, like Syrah except not as gentle. It's most popular as the base for blends in the south of France, but it also makes powerful reds in Sardinia (where it's called Carignano), and a few great examples come from California. (Check out Ridge and Cline, in particular.)

- **Mourvèdre** beats out Syrah in blackness and matches it in spice and earthy herbal notes. To taste it, look for wines from Bandol, France, or examples from California.

- **Sagrantino's** blood-red juice holds red and black-fruit flavors spiked with tannin. It's delicious, powerful stuff native to Umbria, Italy; look for wines labeled Sagrantino di Montefalco (and be ready to pay $20 or more.)

Zinfandel's Rivals

Zinfandel's range is huge, from sweet pink nothings to black monoliths. However, good Zins all share a relaxed, easy edge and a feisty kick of spice. These grapes can't fill in for it, but they are rewarding in their own rights:

- **Agiorgitiko,** like Zinfandel, can make everything from pale pink to black-as-night reds, and all possess a powerful dose of black-cherry flavor. Some are easy drinks; others are built to last decades. All, however, are found under the name of the appellation where they thrive: Nemea, Greece.

- **Corvina** is the grape of Valpolicella in northern Italy. In its lightest forms, its deeply purple juice can stand in for a basic Zinfandel. As an Amarone di Valpolicella, in which the grapes are partially dried to give the wine more intense flavor, it can match up to a bigger, brawnier example.

- **Malbec** is a synonym for Cot, which makes hard, tannic wines in France (see Cabernet Sauvignon, earlier in this chapter), but it tastes completely different in Argentina, where it's the country's best grape. Its licorice-edged black-fruit flavors and smooth but substantial tannins seem designed to match the country's beef. Some reach $50, but great values can be had for around $10.

- **Nero d'Avola** wines tend to be as black as warm-climate Zinfandel, with warm, plum jam flavors balanced by pleasantly raspy tannins. Look for it in Sicilian wines.

I've just described a lot of red wine, but would you want to miss much of it? And there's more where these came from, and from other places we haven't even touched on. Wine can take you on an armchair tour of the world—all it takes is an open mind and an open mouth.

Chapter 14

All That Sparkles

In This Chapter

- How the bubbles get in there
- Deciphering the labels
- Where to find the best

What would life be without sparkling wines? They add an extra celebratory detail to weddings and birthdays; their bubbles brighten up the darkest Monday. Few wines can compete with their versatility at the table, especially when you consider that the options range from dry to sweet, pale to dark red. Don't wait for a special occasion: Bubbles come in handy all the time.

How Do They Get the Bubbles in There?

Sparkling wine, at its most basic, is wine with bubbles. That means it had to be wine first, and then the bubbles were added. How they get in there depends on how much time and money the vintner is willing to spend.

Force It

The easiest way to get bubbles into sparkling wine is to force them—literally. In what's referred to as the "bicycle pump method," the vintner simply injects carbon dioxide into the wine and bottles it under pressure, like a soft drink. The wine bubbles when opened—often violently—but those bubbles don't last long. To keep them longer, sparkling wines need a little more care, as they get in the "tank method."

Tank It

In the tank method (also called *Charmat* after the Frenchman who invented the process in 1907, or *cuve close* in French), wine is put into a pressurized tank, and yeast and sugar are added to provoke a second fermentation, which makes the bubbles. The bubbling wine is then bottled under pressure to retain those bubbles.

This is the most popular way to make affordable sparkling wines, and the result can be pretty good, with fine bubbles that last well. The finest, longest-lasting bubbles, though, are typically achieved by making sparkling wines the traditional way.

Do It the Old-Fashioned Way

The traditional method, or *méthode traditionelle*, is the one used in Champagne, the apex of sparkling wines. As in the tank method, yeast and sugar are added to wine, but before the wine begins to ferment again, the vintner puts the wines into glass bottles and caps them with a crown cap, like the caps on beer bottles.

The bottles are traditionally held in an A-shape frame called a riddling rack. While the wine slowly ferments in the bottle, a riddler comes in daily to turn the bottles, moving them slowly into an upside-down position. (Today many wineries use machines instead of people.) That way, the lees—the dead yeast particles and such—will fall into the neck of the wine, where they can be more easily removed.

Once the bottles are upside down, the vintner freezes the necks of the bottles and opens them. The plug of frozen lees flies out, and he quickly tops up the bottles with a bit of sugar and wine called a *dosage*. Then he corks them and, for an extra bit of security, secures the cork with a wire cage.

Winespeak

The **dosage** is the liquid used to top up the Champagne after the lees are removed from the bottle. It's usually a mixture of sugar and wine or, sometimes, brandy. The sweeter the dosage, the sweeter the Champagne. We'll go into how to figure out the sweetness of a Champagne later in the chapter.

The wine isn't ready for sale yet. It took at least 15 months to get this far, and it'll be another few months or even years before the flavors have melded enough that the wine is ready to be released for sale.

What's the advantage to such a long, arduous process? The longer the wine takes to ferment, and the longer it sits together with the lees, the more flavor it develops. Tinier bubbles are another nice side effect.

Key Terms

When you go to pick out a sparkling wine, you'll notice that many of them, whether French or not, have French terms on them. Some of them have vintage dates; others don't. Here's what's important to know:

Vintage vs. Nonvintage

Like any wines, those that have a vintage date on them must come from the harvest of a single year. In Champagne, great vintages come about only a few times a decade, so when the region does have a great vintage, its producers like to make the most of it with a vintage bottling.

The vintage wine is special; it's a vinous snapshot of the harvest year. However, it's not necessarily better than nonvintage wines. Most sparkling wines are blended from many different vintages; the older vintages help give the wines a deeper, richer flavor, and blending also allows the winery to keep the style of a sparkling wine consistent from one year to the next.

Another difference: Nonvintage sparkling wines are typically ready to be drunk as soon as they are purchased; vintage wines taste better after they've aged for a few years. So if you're buying for tonight or for a consistent flavor you know and like, stick with the nonvintage wine.

Blanc des What?

Blanc des Blancs (*blahnk* day *blahnk*) means "white of whites"; it's a white wine from white grapes. Typically, the white grape is Chardonnay, so the wine emphasizes the lean, sharp, mineral tones of Chardonnay grown in cool areas.

Blanc des Noirs (*blahnk* day *nwoir*) means "white of black," inferring that the wine is a white wine made from red grapes. Traditionally, those grapes are Pinot Noir and/or a relative called Pinot Meunier. They do not have a red color because the vintner removes the grape skins, which hold the color pigments, from the juice directly after pressing. They do sometimes have a hint of red-fruit flavor and a little deeper, darker flavor than Blanc de Blancs.

Rosé sparkling wines can be made either by letting the skins of red grapes soak in the juice long enough to lend it a little color or by adding some still red wine to the blend. Some have lots of red-fruit flavor; others only hint at it.

Extra Confusing

Almost all sparkling wines carry an indication of how sweet the wine is inside. Unfortunately, the designations couldn't be more confusing. They are, from bone-dry to dessert-sweet:

- Brut Nature (or Brut Zéro, Pas Dosé, or Sans-Dosage)
- Extra Brut/Brut Extra
- Brut
- Extra Dry/Extra Sec
- Sec/Dry
- Demi-Sec
- Doux

How "sec," which means dry in French, came to mean "sweet" I can't explain; just remember that if you want a nonsweet sparkling wine, look for the word *brut* on the label.

Choices, Choices

When it comes to sparkling wine, there's one place on the tip of everyone's tongue: Champagne. Champagne is the name of a place in northern France, and only wines made from grapes that grew in this region are truly Champagne. The region's wines, however, have inspired vintners all over the world to try their hand at sparkling wines, the result being a whole lot of great bubbly to try at all different price points.

Champagne

The wine we know as Champagne started as a case of making lemonade out of lemons. The region, which is northeast of Paris, is so cold that often its grapes don't get fully ripe. The tart grapes make mouth-puckeringly sour still wines but offer the right amount of acidity and tartness to balance out the added sugar that's needed to make a sparkling wine.

The results are so delicious that Champagne has set the formula for sparkling wines around the world. That formula is:

Grapes (Chardonnay, Pinot Noir, and/or Pinot Meunier)

+

The time-consuming *méthode traditionelle*

The results within Champagne are wines that are at once bright and refreshing, fruity and toasty, mineral-studded and creamy, with fine, tiny bubbles.

But there are good sparkling wines made outside of Champagne, too.

French Alternatives

Other places in France make wines using the same grape varieties and methods as Champagne:

- **Crémants** can come from anywhere in France, but they must be made using the same grape varieties and methods as Champagne.
- **Blanquette de Limoux** comes from the hills of Limoux, in the northwest Languedoc. Traditionally made from the local white grape Mauzac, it's a light and crisp sparkler.

- **Clairette de Die** grows around the town of Die in the southern Rhône; its lightly floral flavors make for pretty summer pours.

All of these styles of French sparklers can be terrific buys; most run $10 to $30, compared to Champagnes, which start at $25 and run more than $200, with the best values falling in the $40-to-$75 range.

Spanish Sparkling

Head south from France over the Pyrenees, and you'll find Spaniards drinking their own bubbly wine, called Cava.

The Spanish use their own trinity of grapes for Cava: Macabeo, Xarel-lo, and Viura, but they use the same method as Champagne makers (called *método tradicional* in Spanish).

Quick Sip

Cava names to know:

Castillo Perelada

Freixenet

Jaume Serra

Segura Viudas

The final wines are fruity and yeasty, like green apples and fresh-risen bread, and they tend to be amazingly affordable: $8 to $12 buys good examples; add on another $10 for something truly great. In Barcelona, people drink Cava like the Americans do beer: after work, with a snack. It's a tradition we ought to think about adopting in the States.

Italian Sparklers

Italy offers a variety of sparkling wines, from sweet little nothings to strident, lean, mineral-laden wines with bubbles like laser beams. The standouts, however, number just two:

- **Prosecco**—Made in the Veneto region in northern Italy from the Prosecco grape, these sparkling wine are light and fruity, perfect for sipping on warm days and for party pours. Check out Nino Franco, Mionetto, and Zardetto for great $8-to-$15 buys.

- **Franciacorta**—Made in Lombardy from Pinot Grigio and vinified in the same way as Champagne, Franciacorta sparklers are the country's most ambitious, with prices to match. With high acidity, strong minerality, and very dry flavors, they are wines meant more for the dinner table than for sipping.

American Bubbly

Sparkling wines are made all over North and South America. Argentina and Chile put out some crisp, simple examples; Maui uses pineapples to achieve a fruity sparkler. The Gruet family in New Mexico makes fabulous Champagne-like sparklers, and Roman Roth makes fine bubbles at Wölffer Estate on Long Island, New York. No place, however, makes more consistently good sparkling wines than California.

California's cool valleys are so fit for sparkling wine production that Champagne producers such as Mumm (Mumm Napa Valley), Chandon (Domaine Chandon), Roederer (Roederer Estate), and Deutz (Maison Deutz, now Laetitia) have set up shop there, joining Americans such as Iron Horse, J Vineyards and Winery, and Schramsberg. The Spanish have also come, with Gloria Ferrer and Cordoniu (Artesa).

California sparkling wine can be very fine, with crisp, fresh, bright fruit flavors enriched by yeasty lees and mineral notes, but they somehow taste more sunny, a little richer in the fruit department than anything out of Champagne, a little gentler and more easy-going than the wines from Champagne's cold climes.

They also tend to be more affordable, with good versions running about $20, and great ones topping out at $80. Not bad compared to big-name Champagnes, no?

Chapter 15

Sweet Endings

In This Chapter

- Sweet sparklers
- Golden elixirs
- Nutty, caramel-rich pours
- Sweet, sumptuous reds

Sweet wines are an entertainer's best friend. Pull a light, sparkling wine out of the fridge for an impromptu celebration; pour a richer version after dinner when there isn't time to bake a cake. Their sweet flavors can stand in for dessert or make surprisingly delicious accompaniments to savory starters. They might seem expensive at first glance, but remember: A little sweetness goes a long way.

Light, Fizzy, and Sweet

Few desserts are as refreshing on a hot summer's day as a glass of lightly sparkling wine, served chilled. And there is no wine that goes better with birthday or wedding cake. Only a few places do sweet bubblies well, and they are well worth noting.

Italy

Not surprisingly from the country that coined the phrase "la dolce vita," Italy puts out some of the most joyful sweet sparklers. They come in three basic types:

- Moscato d'Asti
- Brachetto d'Acqui
- Lambrusco

Moscato d'Asti comes from Piedmont, where cool temperatures keep the Muscat lightly sweet, redolent of white peaches and flowers. With the addition of bubbles, the Muscat feels light as air and makes a marvelous ending to a heavy meal. It's also delicious poured over peaches.

Brachetto and Lambrusco both make sparkling reds: Brachetto's are lighter and more strawberry-like, while Lambrusco is deep purple with grapey tones. Both are fun for the holidays, and they make good matches with chocolate desserts.

France

The country that claims the invention of sparkling wines offers an array of excellent sweet sparklers. They are typically denoted by the terms *demi-sec* (half-dry), *doux* (sweet), and *moelleux* (marrow, as in soft and rich as warm bone marrow), in increasing order of sweetness. To find them, look particularly to …

- Champagne.
- Loire (Vouvray).

Champagne's Demi-Sec wines are the stuff of weddings and celebrations needing a sweet note, with fine bubbles and bright, appley flavors. The Loire's *pétillant* (sparkling) moelleux wines, on the other hand, are more fitting for sumptuous first courses of pâtés and foie gras because they are made from the honeyed, high-acid Chenin Blanc.

Honey-Sweet and Still

The easiest way to make a sweet wine is to just let the grapes hang on the vines until they are full of sugary sweetness. These wines are called "late-harvest" wines, and they're the most common sweet wines around.

Any kind of grape can be harvested late, so styles range from light whites to deep reds. Here, however, are some of the standouts.

Riesling's Ethereal Sweetness

The best candidates for late-harvest wines are those grapes with the highest acidity—in which case, Riesling is number one. It's turned into sweet wines all over the world, but the most famous are those from Germany. To find light, sweet German Riesling, look for wines marked Auslese (*ows*-lays-uh), which are picked a little later and pack in a bit more fruit.

Off the Vine

Some vintners wait so long to pick their grapes that they freeze on the vine. That makes for painfully cold harvesting, but it's worth the trouble because when the frozen grapes are pressed, all that comes out is nearly pure sugar syrup. Intense? You bet. Delicious? And how. Expensive? Oh yeah. There's not much squeezable juice in a frozen grape. Germany wrote the book on it and calls it Eiswein. Ontario, Canada, and Washington State put out a few, too.

Good late-harvested Rieslings are also made in Australia, Chile, and California.

Chenin's Sumptuousness

If you want more sumptuousness than Riesling offers, try Chenin Blanc. It also has plenty of acidity, but its naturally honeyed flavors and rich, almost unctuous texture make for wines that feel richer. Examples are made from California to South Africa, but, as with the dry versions, they reach their apex in France's Loire, particularly in the appellations Coteaux du Layon, Montlouis, and Quarts du Chaume.

Viognier's Peachy Pleasures

There's not much sweet Viognier in the world, but what exists is worth trying if you can afford it. The grape excels in Condrieu, a small pocket of steep vineyards in the northern Rhône Valley. When left on the vine long into the fall, it takes on weighty flavors of honeyed peaches and apricots, a creamy texture, and a sweet, floral fragrance. These Vendage Tardive examples are delicious enough to bathe in, if only it didn't cost $60 or more. The few examples out of California and Australia don't offer much savings.

Gewürztraminer's Spiced Sweets

Gewürztraminer's naturally spicy flavors make for exotic, heady wines when they are left on the vine to get extra sweet. Versions are made around the world, but Germany and Alsace make the most prized examples.

Gold and Nobly Rotted

It sounds weird, but some of the most prized sweet wines in the world come from rotted grapes. The rot is called botrytis, and when it attacks a grape, it sucks out all the water, leaving a shriveled, sugary berry. Those berries make for intensely sweet wines with complex notes of smoke, honey, and spice from the botrytis.

Botrytized Berries

To try these wines, look for wines from …

- Sauternes (the most famous and pricey).
- Loupiac and Cadillac (nearby appellations, less costly).
- Beerenauslese (BA) and Trockenbeerenauslese (TBA), from Germany.
- Selection de Grains Nobles (SGN), from Alsace.
- Ausbruch wines, from Austria.

None of these wines will be cheap. Waiting for botrytis is risky because there's no guarantee that it will come, and there's every opportunity for the wrong sorts of rot, plus birds, bees, and animals to attack the grapes. And picking botrytis grapes is sticky, hard work, necessitating many passes through the vineyard and lots of work in the winery separating the bad rot from the good. Thought about that way, and tasting the shimmering, sweet results, the prices seem not so bad.

Hungary's Unique Elixir

Vintners in Tokaj, Hungary, combine the smoky richness of botrytised grapes with the fresh-fruit sweetness of late-harvest grapes in one wine, called Tokaji (with an *i*). They do this by smashing all the botrytized grapes and storing them in a container called a *puttonyo*. Then a number of puttonyos of mashed grapes are added to the juice of unbotry-tised grape and left to macerate together. The sweetness of the final wine depends on how many puttonyos of wine went in, which is marked on the label. Three is most common, and fairly sweet; seven is rare and thick, with sweet, smoky flavor.

Most Tokaji run about $40 to $80, which doesn't seem bad for a wine that was known before communism as "the wine of kings" and that can last in the cellar for a century.

Caramel-Rich and Dark

Some parts of the world like their sweet wines rich and dark, like vinous versions of caramel. To achieve this, vintners often dry the grapes a little bit before pressing them. The reduced juice comes out dark and thick.

In France, these wines are called *vin de paille*, or straw wines, named after the straw mats on which they dry.

In Italy, the most famous are called Vinsanto and come from Tuscany, where the spicy, nutty, golden wines come in handy for dunking biscotti. There are also affordable versions from the island of Pantelleria, off of Sicily. These are made from Muscat that's dried on mats for a month; they taste like golden raisins wrapped in honey. Harder to find are Recioto wines from the Veneto, although the sweet, spiced plum flavors of a red Recioto della Valpolicella are worth seeking out for chocolate desserts.

Fortified Wines

There's another way to make sweet wines, and that's to kill the yeasts in a fermenting wine with extra alcohol so the wine stops fermenting away its sugars. The finished wines have a bit more alcohol than most and potently sweet fresh flavors. They can be made from all sorts of grapes, but the major categories are sketched out here, from lightest to richest.

Orange Blossoms and Golden Raisins

In the south of France, vintners have long been adding alcohol to their wines to keep them sweet and to protect them from the intense heat. They call their fortified wines *vin doux naturel*, commonly abbreviated to VDN. These are the major styles:

- **Muscat de Beaumes de Venise**—Grown in the Southern Rhône, this is the lightest, most delicate, with orange-blossom scents and flavors.

- **Muscat de Frontignan**—Darker in color and flavor, as if warmed more by the more intense sun and heat in its home, the Languedoc.

- **Rivesaltes**—Grown on the hot, sun-soaked coast of Roussillon, these dark Muscats have toasty orange and nut flavors.

Australia also makes many sweet, fortified Muscats, which they commonly call "stickies." If you've ever had a caramel-drenched sticky pudding, you know why. These are intensely sweet and caramel-thick, with golden raisin flavors.

Cherry Ripe and Sweet

Grenache's sweet red-cherry flavors are a natural for turning into sweet wines. The French, in fact, have made a habit of it in these places:

- Banyuls (Roussillon)
- Maury (Roussillon)

Banyuls is rich, with heady cherry sweetness mixed with vanilla and spice. Maury is even richer, with such deep, chocolate-cherry flavors that one vintner joined forces with French chocolatier Valrhona to package the chocolate with his wines. Since chocolate is typically difficult to pair with wine, these are essential wines for chocoholics to know about.

Port Pleasures

Sweet reds reach their apex in Portugal, which gave its name to Port. There are a few sweet white Ports, but red is where it's at. Grown along the hot, precipitously steep slopes of the Douro Valley in Portugal, Port is like bottled sun—sweet, warm, and condensed into an opaque purple juice.

Quick Sip

Only wines from Portugal's Douro Valley are real Ports, but other countries make good Port-style wines. Look especially for sweet Zinfandels from California, which match Ports in size and sweet purple fruit, if not in complexity.

When buying Port, you'll be faced with an array of choices. The most important thing to know is that Port is usually made from a blend of vintages. Only in exceptional years will Port producers "declare" a vintage and bottle vintage-dated wines. That understood, here's what the terms mean:

- **Ruby**—The simplest, freshest Port, blended from one- to three-year-old wines

- **Vintage Character**—A step up from Ruby, with slightly richer flavors

- **Late Bottled Vintage (LBV)**—A wine made from the harvest of a single vintage that was good, but not great enough to declare, and aged four to six years to mellow

- **Single Quinta**—Made from the grapes of a single vineyard, or quinta

- **Vintage**—Made from the grapes of a single, excellent harvest, the year of which always appears on the label

The first three styles of Port are typically ready to drink as soon as they are purchased. Single Quinta and Vintage wines, however, need to be cellared for years before they reach their peak. If you want the flavor of a well-aged Port but can't wait 10 or 20 years, then look for …

- Tawny Port.
- Colheita Port.

Both Tawny and Colheita Ports are aged in wooden casks for years before bottling so that they become tawny in color and taste. The longer the wine stays in a cask, the less fruity and more nutty it becomes. Better Tawny Ports have an indication of age on the label, as in "10 Year Old"; the number is the average age of the wines inside. Colheita Ports are from a single year, so they will have a vintage date on the label.

Sherry's Range

Sherry is also a fortified wine, but it's not like anything else. Although lots of people think Sherry is an old lady's drink, it's actually one of the most complex, unusual wines on the planet. It's made in Jerez, on the hot southern coast of Spain, from super-ripe, superacidic grapes that are pressed and their juice put it into wooden casks to ferment.

That juice grows a film of yeast, called *flor*, on its surface, which contributes to Sherry's particular taste. And when it's finished fermenting, it gets put into a solera, a pyramid of casks each holding older wines. The youngest wine goes into the top cask, and as wine is taken out of the bottom casks to be bottled, the bottom casks are replenished with younger wine from the casks above.

This result is wines that taste of nuts and caramel, with a salty edge from the sea air and a yeasty note from the flor. Some, however, are bone dry; others are as sweet as maple syrup. In ascending order of sweetness, the seven styles available are Fino, Manzanilla, Amontillado, Palo Cortado, Oloroso, Cream Sherry, and Pedro Ximenez (often called PX).

If you're looking for a dessert Sherry, look for Oloroso or above. Some PXs are so thick that they are best served by the eyedropper full or drizzled over vanilla ice cream. All, however, are bargains because so many people ignore them. Their loss, your gain—like so many of the wines in this book. Cheers!

The World's Great Grapes by Country

There are lots of great wines in the world, but some varieties excel in certain countries. Here's a crib sheet to the most exciting grape varieties in each country or region:

Argentina: Malbec (red), Torrontès (wh)

Australia: Shiraz (red)

Austria: Grüner Veltliner, Riesling (wh)

California: Chardonnay (wh); Cabernet Sauvignon, Zinfandel (reds)

Chile: Carmenère (red), Sauvignon Blanc (wh)

France: Chardonnay (wh); Cabernet Sauvignon, Merlot, Pinot Noir, Syrah (reds); blends (wh & red)

Germany: Riesling (wh)

Greece: Assyrtiko (wh); Agiorgitiko, Xinomavro (reds)

Italy: Pinot Grigio, Tocai Friulano, Vermentino (wh); Barbera, Dolcetto, Nebbiolo, Sangiovese (reds)

New York State: Riesling (wh), Pinot Noir (red)

New Zealand: Sauvignon Blanc (wh), Pinot Noir (red)

Oregon: Pinot Gris (wh); Pinot Noir (red)

Portugal: Baga, Touriga Franca, Touriga Nacional (reds)

South Africa: Pinotage (red), Sauvignon Blanc (wh)

Spain: Garnacha, Tempranillo (reds)

Washington State: Merlot (red)

The Grapes Behind the Names

Many of the Old World's great wines don't list the grape variety on the label. Don't let that stop you: Use this list to figure out what the major grape(s) are in each of these common wines.

Italy

Barolo and **Barbaresco**   Nebbiolo

Chianti   Sangiovese

France

Beaujolais   Gamay

Bourgueil   Cabernet Franc

Burgundy, white   Chardonnay

Burgundy, red   Pinot Noir

Bordeaux, white   Sauvignon Blanc and Semillon

Bordeaux, red   Cabernet Sauvignon and Merlot

Chablis   Chardonnay

Champagne   Pinot Noir and Chardonnay

Chinon   Cabernet Franc

Pouilly-Fumé   Sauvignon Blanc

Pouilly-Fuissé   Chardonnay

Quincy   Sauvignon Blanc

Rhône Valley, northern   Syrah

Rhône Valley, southern   Syrah plus Grenache, Mourvèdre, and others

Sancerre, white   Sauvignon Blanc

Sancerre, red   Pinot Noir

Savennières   Chenin Blanc

Vouvray   Chenin Blanc

Spain

Priorat   Grenache, known in Spanish as Garnacha

Ribera del Duero   Tempranillo, here called Tinto Fino

Rioja   Tempranillo

Appendix C

Breaking Down the Jargon

You don't need to talk the talk to enjoy wine, but you will encounter plenty of people who do. Here's a quick guide to the terms you might read in wine books or overhear at wine stores or tastings.

acetic   Like vinegar. Not good.

acidify   To add acid, which actually can be purchased by the bag. It happens often, though vintners don't often like to admit it.

ageability   Not a word, according to spell-check, but frequently heard to describe a wine that someone thinks can get better over many years.

appellation   The place from which the wine came.

astringent   Drying, tannic.

ausbruch   Austrian term for sweet wines made with botrytised grapes.

auslese   A German designation of ripeness, typically, but not always, indicating a sweet wine.

austere   Dry, stony, lean; not fruity, not rich in flavor.

AVA   American Viticultural Area, the official designation for a defined geographical area for grape growing in the United States.

barnyard   A polite way of saying a wine smells faintly like animal excrement. Not always a bad thing.

battonage   French for the act of stirring the lees to extract more flavor from them.

beads   A poetic metaphor for the bubbles in a sparkling wine.

beerenauslese   Second-highest designation of ripeness in the German Prädikat scheme, and indicating sweet wines made from botrytised grapes.

big   Lots of flavor; mouth-filling.

Blanc des Blancs   A white wine made from white grapes. Most often used in sparkling wines.

Blanc des Noirs   A white wine made from red grapes. Most often used in sparkling wines.

Bocksbeutel   A squat, round bottle traditionally used by vintners in the regions of Franken and northern Baden in Germany.

body   How light or heavy a wine feels in the mouth.

bouquet   Particularly pretentious word for "scent."

Bourgogne Rouge   French for red Burgundy, a Pinot Noir wine; *Bourgogne Blanc* means white Burgundy, a wine made from Chardonnay.

botrytis cinerea   A good rot, also called "noble rot." It gives sweet wines extra concentration and adds a smoky, honeyed flavor.

bottle stink   The rubbery smell that sometimes comes off a glass of wine poured from a bottle that's just been open. It will go away with a few minutes in the glass.

Brettanomyces   A yeast that can make a wine smell a little like sweat, wet dog, or sweaty horse. In small amounts, it can add pleasantly interesting notes to a wine.

chaptalization   The addition of sugar to a wine. Not legal everywhere.

corked   Infected with TCA, a bacteria that makes wine smell like wet cardboard.

crémant   French term indicating sparkling wine made by the traditional method used in Champagne, but made outside Champagne's boundaries.

crisp   High acid.

cru   Means "growth," in the sense of "vineyard." A Grand Cru wine, for instance, comes from a "great growth," or a vineyard recognized as producing great wines.

cuvée   French for a blend.

decant   To transfer a wine into a larger container, traditionally for the purpose of separating the wine from the sediment in the bottom of the bottle, or to aerate the wine, but also often done to look fancy.

deep   Having lots of flavors that seem to last a long time and keep changing in the mouth.

disgorge   To take out, typically used to refer to the process of removing the sediment from the neck of a Champagne bottle.

DO or **Denominación de Origen** The Spanish appellation system.

DOC Denominación de Origen Calificada, Denominacão de Origem Controlada, Denominazione di Origine Controllata; the Spanish, Portuguese, and Italian (in that order) appellation systems.

dosage The small amount of wine and sugar added to a sparkling wine after it has been disgorged and before it is corked for the last time. The sweetness of the dosage affects the sweetness of the final wine.

earthy Tastes of the earth in a pleasant way, like the smell of warm dirt or of sun-baked earth. Not the same as muddy.

Edelzwicker A term used in Alsace to identify a wine made from a blend of two or more of Gewürztraminer, Muscat, Pinot Blanc, Pinot Gris, Pinot Noir, and Sylvaner.

Eiswein German for supersweet wines made from grapes that have frozen on the vine.

enologist Person who has studied winemaking.

Erstes Gewächs "First Growth" in German, a designation sometimes used in the Rheingau meant to signify the very best vineyards of the region.

exposition The position of a vineyard, in terms of angle, sun, and altitude.

fat A wine with lots of fruity flavor and not so much tannin or acidity.

filtered Run through a filter to remove debris.

fined Cleaned up of very small particles of debris, with an addition of a protein that attracts the particles.

finish   The aftertaste.

flabby   Blah, all fruit and no zest; lacks acidity.

fortified wine   Wine to which extra alcohol has been added, such as Port, Sherry, and Vin Doux Naturel.

foxy   Tastes like a fox—or what you'd imagine a fox to taste like. Common description for wines made out of vitis labrusca grapes, such as Concords.

fresh   Full of life.

frizzante   Lightly bubbly, in Italian.

Fruit-Loopy   Smells like Froot Loops, no joking. Happens to some fruity white wines. Professionals often call it "linalool."

garrigue   A French term used to describe the mix of fragrant wild herbs and brush common to the Mediterranean countryside that sometimes turns up in the scent of wines from Southern France.

Gewürz   Spice in German; it's also shorthand for Gewürztraminer, the grape.

gooseberry   A round, tart fruit with a distinctive taste, very common in England. It's worth trying; the flavor is similar to that of many Sauvignon Blancs.

Grand Cru   "Great growth" in French, applied to vineyards that have proven over time to produce exceptional wines.

grapey   Tastes like fresh-pressed grapes. See? This is easy!

grassy   Tastes like fresh-cut green grass.

green   Unripe. Can come through as green peppers; herbs; or unripe plums, strawberries, or any other fruit you'd rather eat when it's totally ripe. Fine in small amounts; not good when exaggerated.

green harvest To prune grapes from the vine before harvest, in the hopes that the vine will concentrate its energy on the remaining grapes.

late harvest Harvested late in the season, when the grapes are very ripe.

laying down Putting away a bottle to age (usually on its side).

legs A very un-P.C. term for the glycerous trails left on the side of a glass after swirling the wine. The longer the legs, the richer the wine. *Also see* tears.

length, as in "has nice length." Means the flavor lasts a while.

linalool *See* Fruit-Loopy.

maceration To let the grape skins and juice soak together to extract flavor.

maderized Tastes like Madeira but isn't, which is usually a sign that the wine has turned brown and nutty from exposure to oxygen.

malolactic fermentation A second fermentation in which hard malic acid is turned into softer lactic acid. Also called ML.

Meritage An official term used in the United States to designate wines that are made from a blend of traditional Bordeaux varieties.

méthode champenoise The technique used to make Champagne in Champagne, France. Also called méthode traditionelle.

méthode traditionelle   Made in the same way as Champagne.

mineral   Tastes like metal or stone—hard to describe, which is why the word is pretty vague.

moelleux   French for "marrow," used to indicate a medium-sweet wine.

mousseaux   French for bubbly wine.

MS   Master Sommelier, a person who has passed a difficult exam on wine and wine service.

muddy   Can infer that the wine tastes of mud or that the flavors are thick and indistinct. Neither are positives.

must   The mashed-up grapes before fermentation.

MW   Master of Wine, a person who has passed an exam that tests knowledge of wine and the business of wine.

new world   The parts of the world that haven't been making wine in a big way for more than a couple hundred years, such as the Americas, Australia, New Zealand, and South Africa.

noble rot   *See* botrytis.

nose   Silly way to refer to the scent of the wine. "This wine has a very fine nose" equals "Smells good."

oaky   Tastes of vanilla, spice, and/or straight, fresh-sawed wood. Good wines taste of fruit, with only hints of wood; many wines, however, taste more like wood than fruit.

oenologist   A person who studies wine. Also spelled *enologist*.

oenology The study of wine. Also spelled *enology*.

off-dry Strangely, this means the wine is a little bit sweet.

old world The parts of the world that have been making wine on a major scale for several hundred years at the least, such as Europe and the Middle East.

oxidized Turned brown in color and nutty in flavor due to exposure to oxygen. Can be good or bad, depending on context and your fondness for nutty, dried-fruit flavors.

palate The roof of your mouth, though it's used incorrectly all the time by wine geeks instead of "mouth," as in, "Tastes fruity on the palate."

passito Italian term to indicate wine made from dried grapes.

pearls Retro, poetic term for the bubbles in wine.

peppery Can mean many things, from a pleasant, fresh-crushed black pepper–like spice to the green note of a jalapeño. Often, however, it's a polite way of saying the wine's alcohol burns, like too much white pepper does in a dish.

pétillant Delicate French term for lightly sparkling.

phylloxera A nasty vine aphid that sucks the life out of grapevines through their roots.

Prädikat German for "distinction," a designation of ripeness of grapes at harvest in German wines. Includes, in ascending order of ripeness, Kabinett, Spätlese, Auslese, Beerenauslese, and Trockenbeerenauslese.

rancio   Indicates a wine that has been exposed to the elements, giving it the nutty flavors of oxidation.

R.D.   "Recently disgorged," used in sparkling wines to indicate a wine that was left on the lees for an extended time to pick up extra flavor and complexity. Also called, confusingly, L.D., or "late disgorged."

recioto   A wine made from dried grapes; typical to Italy's Veneto region.

reserva   Spanish for "reserve," and used to indicate a wine that has had more aging than nonreserva wines.

reserve   Typically indicates a wine of higher quality than nonreserve wines, although the term has no legal meaning in the United States.

residual sugar, or RS   Any sugar left in the wine when it's done fermenting. Much fuss is made over RS, but in fact, a wine with 7 grams per liter of RS can taste drier than one with just 3 grams but less acidity. Taste is your best measure of the sweetness of a wine.

ripasso   Literally to repass, used to describe wines that are made by passing the wine a second time over the skins left over from pressing, making a richer wine.

rosado   "Pink" in Spanish.

Rosé   "Pink" in French, and frequently used on its own worldwide to indicate pink wine.

sec   French for "dry," though sec Champagne is actually sweet. Go figure.

second-label wines   Wines a winery makes under a different label than its flagship wines, typically more affordable but still of good quality.

Sekt   German sparkling wine.

Sélection de Grains Nobles   French term used in Alsace to describe wines made from botrytised grapes.

sommelier   The person responsible for the wines in a restaurant—and that includes helping you pick them.

Spätburgunder   Pinot Noir in German.

spumante   Sparkling wine, in Italian, more bubbly than frizzante wines.

Steen   South African name for Chenin Blanc.

stemmy   Like chewing on grape stems, which are usually a little green and bitter-tasting.

stony   Not fruity; instead, tastes more like a stone smells.

structure   The acidity and tannin that give a wine shape and make it feel lively and interesting instead of flabby and dull.

sulfites   The salts left over from sulfur dioxide.

Super-Tuscan   Pumped-up wines from Tuscany, Italy. It was invented to describe Tuscan wines that, because they were made with untraditional grapes, had to take the lowly "vino da tavola" designation and yet fetched high praise and high prices in the marketplace.

sur lie   "On the lees," a phrase that indicates that the wine stayed in contact with the lees for an extended period of time before bottling.

table wine   In general, these are wines you'd serve for a casual dinner. In the United States, it means simply that the wine is dry; elsewhere, it often indicates dry wines of very basic quality.

tannins The stuff in red wines that makes your mouth feel dry and scratchy, like oversteeped tea does. That sounds bad, but in fact, tannins help preserve a wine, and many tannic wines will last well for years, becoming less tannic and more complex.

tartrates A by-product of tartaric acid that often leaves small, harmless crystals on the end of the cork or the bottom of the bottle.

TCA The bacteria that makes wines taste "corked," or like wet cardboard.

tears A poetic reference to the drips of wine left on the side of a wine glass after it has been swirled.

terroir The flavor of a place brought about by its particular arrangement of natural influences.

texture How a wine feels in the mouth, such as silky, rough, satiny, or prickly.

tight Not showing much flavor, but having the feel of lots of tannins and acidity.

tinto "Red" in Spanish and Portuguese.

toasty Tasting of toast, or of toasted wood, usually a result of time spent in toasted oak barrels.

trocken "Dry" in German. Unlike *sec* in France, *trocken* always indicates a dry wine.

Trockenbeerenauslese A wine that's reached the highest level of ripeness in the German designation scheme and that is made from grapes that have been infected with botrytis.

unfiltered A wine that has not been run through any filters to remove particles that could possibly cause the wine to spoil. Some people think filtering removes flavor as well as particles.

unfined A wine that has not been treated with a fining agent, such as egg whites, charcoal, or bentonite, to remove teensy particles from the wine.

uva "Grape" in Italian.

varietal wine A wine made from one variety (or the legal minimum of one variety) and labeled by the name of the grape.

variety The kind of grape—Merlot is a grape variety.

vegetal Smells like vegetables, whether bell peppers or roasted rutabagas or the compost heap. Rather unfortunate characteristic.

vendange tardive Late harvest in French.

viniculture The study of winemaking.

vinify To make into wine.

vintage The year in which a wine was harvested.

vintner The person who makes wine.

viticulture The study of vine growing.

vitis labrusca The species of grape vine native to the United States, prized for eating out of hand far more than for winemaking.

vitis vinifera The species of grape vine responsible for most of the great wines of the world.

volatile A wine that smells a little vinegary.

Index

A

acidity, Riesling, 67-69
Adelaide Hills (Australia),
    Pinot Noir, 117
Africa, Pinotage, 145
Agiorgitiko, 149
Aglianico, 148
ah-so corkscrew, 6
Albariño, 143
Alexander Valley (Sonoma,
    California), Zinfandel, 132
Alsace, France
    Pinot Blanc, 85
    Pinot Grigio, 83-84
    Riesling, 73-74
Alvarinho, 143
amarone, 28
American Viticultural
    Areas. *See* AVAs
Amontillado, 172
appellations, 20-22
Argentina
    Malbec, 150
    Torronte, 141
Arneis, 143
Assyrtiko, 142
Ausbruch wines, 166
Auslese (Prädikat level), 70
Australia
    Cabernet Sauvignon,
        95-96
    Merlot, 106
    Pinot Noir, 116-117
    Sauvignon Blanc, 66
    Syrah, 122-124
Austria
    Riesling, 74-76
    Zweigelt, 147
AVAs (American
    Viticultural Areas), 115

B

back labels (wine bottles), 29
Baga, 145
Banyuls, 169
bar-mounted corkscrews, 7
Barbera, 146
bargain wines, white wines,
    139
Barossa (Australia), Shiraz,
    123
Beerenauslese, 166
Beerenauslese (Prädikat
    level), 70
Beringer Chardonnay, 58
bicycle pump method,
    forcing bubbles in
    sparkling wines, 152
Blanc des Blancs (sparkling
    wines), 155
Blanc des Noirs (sparkling
    wines), 155
Blanquette de Limoux, 157
blended wines, Cabernet
    Sauvignon, 96
blending grapes, 121

Bordeaux, France
    Cabernet Sauvignon,
        90-92
    Merlot, 101-103
botrytized wines, 165-166
Brachetto d'Acqui, 162
brut sparkling wines, 156
bubbles, forcing in
    sparkling wines, 151-154
    bicycle pump method,
        152
    tank method, 152
    traditional method,
        152-154
Burgundy, France
    Chardonnay, 50, 52
    Pinot Noir, 110-113

C

Cabernet Franc, 97
Cabernet Sauvignon
    Australia, 95-96
    blending grapes, 96
    Bordeaux, France, 90-92
    California, 93-95
    costs, 98
    rival wines, 144, 146
    taste variations, 89
    versus Cabernet Franc,
        97
Cadillac, 166
California
    Cabernet Sauvignon,
        93-95
    Chardonnay, 53
    Merlot, 105
    Mourvèdre, 149
    Pinot Noir, 115

    Sauvignon Blanc, 64
    sparkling wines, 160
    Syrah, 124-126
    Zinfandel, 131-134
Cannonau, 147
Canterbury region (New
    Zealand), Pinot Noir, 116
Carignan, 149
Carmenère, 106
Carneros (California),
    Pinot Noir, 115
Casablanca, Chile,
    Sauvignon Blanc, 65
Cat Pee on a Gooseberry
    Bush Sauvignon Blanc, 62
Central Otago region
    (New Zealand), Pinot
    Noir, 116
Chablis (Burgundy,
    France), 51
Champagne, 156-158, 162
Chardonnay, 46
    costs, 57
    ML (malolactic fermen-
        tation), 56-57
    oak flavors, 54
    rival wines, 140
    terroir and minerality,
        49-50
    winegrowing regions,
        46-53
Chassagne-Montrachet
    appellation, 52
Château Mouton-
    Rothschild winery, 92
Châteauneuf-du-Pape
    appellation (Rhône
    Valley), Syrah, 122
Chenin Blanc
    sweet wines, 164
    versus Chardonnay, 140

Chile
  Merlot, 106
  Sauvignon Blanc, 65
Clairette de Die, 158
class distinctions, Cabernet
  Sauvignon, 92
climates
  affects on taste, 146
  cool-climate
    Chardonnay, 47-48
  grape growth and, 18-19
  warm-climate
    Chardonnay, 48
Cline California Zinfandel,
  133
Colheita Port, 171
Cono Sur (Pinot Noir), 118
Constantia, South Africa,
  Sauvignon Blanc, 65
cool-climate Chardonnay,
  47-48
corks
  removing pieces from
    wine, 8
  restaurant wines and, 35
corkscrews, 4-7
  ah-so, 6
  bar-mounted models, 7
  lever pulls, 7
  straight corkscrews, 5
  waiter's friend, 5-6
  winged double-lever
    pulls, 6
Corvina, 150
costs
  Cabernet Sauvignon, 98
  Chardonnay, 57
  Merlot, 107
  Pinot Grigio, 86
  Pinot Noir, 117-118
  restaurant wines, 40-42

Riesling, 76
Shiraz, 123
sparkling wines, 158
Syrah, 121, 127
Cot, 145
Côte-Rôtie appellation
  (Rhône Valley), Syrah, 120
Côte d'Or (Burgundy,
  France), 51
Crémants, 157
Crozes-Hermitage appella-
  tion (Rhône Valley),
  Syrah, 120

D

dessert wines
  botrytized wines,
    165-166
  Chenin Blanc, 164
  fortified wines, 168-171
  Gewürztraminer, 165
  Riesling, 163-164
  Sherry, 171
  sparkling wines, 161-163
  Tokaji, 166-167
  vin de paille, 167
  Vinsanto, 167
  Viognier, 165
Diel, Dönhoff (Nahe), 72
Dolcetto, 146
Domaine Roumier
  Bonnes-Mares vineyard,
  113
Dry Creek Valley (Sonoma,
  California), Zinfandel,
  132
dry wines, trocken, 70

E

Echelon Chardonnay, 58
Eden Valley (Australia),
    Pinot Noir, 117
Edna Valley Vineyard
    Chardonnay, 58
Erath (Pinot Noir), 118

F

Fabre Montmayou Grand
    Vin (Argentina), 97
Falanghina, 142
Federspiel (Wachau
    Riesling), 75
Fiano di Avellino, 143
Fino, 172
food pairings
    dessert wines. *See*
        dessert wines
    restaurant wines, 38-40
    Sauvignon Blanc, 66
forcing bubbles (sparkling
    wines), 151-154
    bicycle pump method,
        152
    tank method, 152
    traditional method,
        152-154
fortified wines
    Grenache, 169
    Ports, 169-171
    Sherry, 171
    VDN (vin doux
        naturel), 168-169
Fox Run (Pinot Noir), 118

France
    Alsace
        Pinot Blanc, 85
        Pinot Grigio, 83-84
        Riesling, 73-74
    Bordeaux's Cabernet
        Sauvignon
    appellations, 91-92
    class distinctions, 92
    Left Bank regions, 90-92
    Premier Cru, 92
    Burgundy's Pinot Noir,
        110-113
    Carignan, 149
    Champagne, 156, 158
    Chardonnay, 50, 52
    Cot, 145
    Loire Sauvignon
        Blancs, 60, 62
    Loire Valley's Pinot
        Noir, 113-114
    Melon, 142
    Merlot, 101-103
    Rhône Valley, Syrah,
        119-122
    sweet wines, 162-163,
        168-169
    Tannat, 145
    vin de paille, 167
Franciacorta, 159
Franken vineyards,
    Riesling, 72
free-run juices, 130
Friuli, Italy
    Pinot Grigio, 82
    Tocai Friulano, 142
Fumé Blanc, 65
Fürst, Schmitts Kinder
    (Franken), 72

G

Gamay, 147
Garnacha, 147
Germany
    Riesling, 69-72, 163-164
    Scheurebe, 142
Gewürztraminer, 141, 165
Gigondas appellation (Rhône
    Valley), Syrah, 122
glassware, 8-9
Grand Cru, 93, 112-113
grapes
    affects of climate on
        growth, 18-19
    blending, 121
    botrytized wines,
        165-166
    free-run juices, 130
    varietals, 23
    varieties, 22-23
Grauburgunder, 80
Greco di Tufo, 143
Greek wines
    Agiorgitiko, 149
    Assyrtiko, 142
    Moskofilero, 141
Grenache, fortified wines,
    169

H

Heartbreak Grape, The, 109
Hermitage appellation
    (Rhône Valley), Syrah, 120
Hungary, Tokaji, 166-167
Hunter Valley (Australia),
    Shiraz, 123

I

icewine, 28
importers, 29
Italy
    Aglianico, 148
    Arneis, 143
    Barbera, 146
    Corvina, 150
    Dolcetto, 146
    Fiano di Avellino, 143
    Greco di Tufo, 143
    Merlot, 105-106
    Montepulciano, 147
    Nebbiolo, 147
    Pinot Grigio, 80-83
    Refosco, 145
    Sagrantino, 149
    Sangiovese, 148
    sparkling wines, 159
    sweet wines, 162
    Tocai Friulano, 142
    Trebbiano, 144
    Verdicchio, 144
    Vinsanto, 167
    Zinfandel, 135

J-K

Joseph Drouhin Charmes-
    Chambertin vineyard, 113
Joseph Drouhin La Fôret
    Bourgogne (Pinot Noir),
    118

Kabinett (Prädikat level), 70
Kamptal vineyards
    (Austria), Riesling, 74
Konstantin Frank (New
    York State Riesling), 76

Kremstal vineyards
  (Austria), Riesling, 74

L

labels. *See* wine labels
Lambrusco, 162
lees, 57
Left Bank region (Bordeaux,
  France), Cabernet
  Sauvignon, 90-92
Leitz, Robert Weil
  (Rheingau), 72
lever pulls corkscrew, 7
Lindemans Bin 99 (Pinot
  Noir), 118
Lirac appellation (Rhône
  Valley), Syrah, 122
Listrac-Médoc appellation
  (Bordeaux, France),
  Cabernet Sauvignon, 91
lists (wine lists)
    finding good deals, 40-41
    food pairings, 38-40
    sommelier's role, 32-33
Lodi (California),
  Zinfandel, 133
Loire, 162
Loire Valley (France)
    Pinot Noir, 113-114
    Sauvignon Blanc, 60-62
Loupiac, 166

M

Malbec, 145, 150
malolactic fermentation.
  See ML

Manzanilla, 172
Marcel Deiss vineyard
  (Alsace, France), Riesling,
  73
Margaux appellation
  (Bordeaux, France),
  Cabernet Sauvignon, 91
Marsanne versus
  Chardonnay, 140
Martinborough region
  (New Zealand), Pinot
  Noir, 116
Maury, 169
Mâcon appellation, 52
Mâconnais (Burgundy,
  France), 51
McLaren Vale (Australia),
  Shiraz, 123
Melon, 142
Mendocino (California),
  Zinfandel, 131-133
Menetou-Salon Sauvignon,
  61
Merlot
    Australia, 106
    California, 105
    Chile, 106
    costs, 107
    Italy, 105-106
    Right Bank Bordeaux
      (France), 101-103
    rival wines, 146-147
    Switzerland, 105
    versus Carmenère, 106
    Washington, 104
Meursault appellation, 52
Mexico, Zinfandel, 135
minerality
    Chardonnay, 49-50
    Riesling, 67-69

ML (malolactic fermentation), Chardonnay, 56-57
Mongeard-Mugneret Echézeaux vineyard, 113
Montepulciano, 147
Moscato d'Asti, 162
Mosel-Saar-Ruwer vineyards, Riesling, 71
Moskofilero, 141
Moulis appellation (Bordeaux, France), Cabernet Sauvignon, 91
Mourvèdre, 149
Muscat, 141
Muscat de Beaumes de Venise, 168
Muscat de Frontignan, 168

N

Nahe vineyards, Riesling, 71
Napa Valley (California)
    Cabernet Sauvignon, 93-95
    Syrah, 125-126
    Zinfandel, 134
Navarro Mendocino (Pinot Noir), 118
Nebbiolo, 147
Nero d'Avola, 150
New Mexico, sparkling wines, 160
new world style wines, 19-20
New York State
    Pinot Noir, 117
    Riesling, 76
New Zealand
    Pinot Noir, 116
    Sauvignon Blanc, 62-64

Nicolas Potel Chambertin vineyard, 113
nonvintage sparkling wines, 154-155
Northern Rhône appellations (France), Syrah, 120-121

O

oaked wines, 54
old vine wines, 132-133
old world style wines, 19-20
Oloroso, 172
opening wine bottles, 4-7
Oregon
    Pinot Grigio, 84-85
    Pinot Noir, 114

P

Paso Robles (California), Zinfandel, 134
Pauillac appellation (Bordeaux, France), Cabernet Sauvignon, 91
Pedro Ximenez, 172
Pessac-Léognan appellation (Bordeaux, France), Cabernet Sauvignon, 91
Petite Sirah, 126-127
Pfalz vineyards, Riesling, 72
pink wines, Zinfandel, 129, 131
Pinot Bianco, 85
Pinot Blanc, 85
Pinot Grigio
    Alsace, France, 83-84
    costs, 86

Italy, 80-83
Oregon, 84-85
styles, 79-80, 86
versus Pinot Bianco, 85
Pinot Gris, 80, 143-144
Pinot Nero, 116
Pinot Noir, 109
  Australia, 116-117
  Burgundy, France,
    110-113
  California, 115
  costs, 117-118
  Loire Valley, France,
    113-114
  New York State, 117
  New Zealand, 116
  Oregon, 114
  rival wines, 147-148
Pinotage, 145
Port, 169, 171
Portugal
  Baga, 145
  Port, 169, 171
  Touriga Nacional, 146
Pouilly-Fuisse appellation, 52
Pouilly-Fume Sauvignon, 61
pouring tips, 10, 37-38
Prädikat levels, 69-70
Premier Cru, 92
Primitivo, 135
Prosecco, 159
Puligny-Montrachet appel-
  lation, 52
PX (Pedro Ximenez), 172

Q-R

quality classifications, 26-28
Quincy Sauvignon, 61

Rasteau appellation (Rhône
  Valley), Syrah, 122
Ravenswood Vintners
  Blend Zinfandel, 133
Red Mountain
  (Washington State),
  Merlot, 104
red wines
  Cabernet Sauvignon,
    89-98, 144-146
  Merlot, 146-147
  Pinot Noir, 109-118,
    147-148
  Syrah, 119-127, 148-149
  Zinfandel, 131-134, 149
Refosco, 145
regional wines
  Cabernet Sauvignon,
    90-96
  Chardonnay, 46-53
  Merlot, 101-106
  Pinot Bianco, 85
  Pinot Grigio, 80-85
  Pinot Noir, 110-117
  Riesling, 69-76
  Sauvignon Blanc, 60-65
  Syrah, 119-127
  Zinfandel, 131-135
restaurant wines
  checking the label, 34
  corks, 35
  food pairings, 38-40
  pouring, 37-38
  tasting, 36
  tipping sommeliers, 42
  wine lists, 32-33, 40-41
Reuilly Sauvignon, 61
Rheingau vineyards,
  Riesling, 72

Rhône Valley, France,
Syrah, 119-122
Ribolla Gialla, 144
Riesling
acidity and minerality,
67-69
Alsace, France, 73-74
Austria, 74-76
costs, 76
Germany, 69-72
New York State, 76
rival wines, 142
sweet wines, 163-164
taste variations, 67-69
Right Bank Bordeaux
(France), Merlot, 101-103
ripasso, 28
rival wines
Cabernet Sauvignon,
144-146
Chardonnay, 140
Merlot, 146-147
Pinot Gris, 143-144
Pinot Noir, 147-148
Riesling, 142
Sauvignon Blanc, 141
Syrah, 148-149
Zinfandel, 149
Rivesaltes, 168
Rosenblum Vintner's
Cuvée Zinfandel, 133
Rosé (sparkling wines), 155
Roussanne, 140
Russian River Valley
(California)
Pinot Noir, 115
Zinfandel, 132

S

Sagrantino, 149
Sancerre Sauvignon, 61
Sangiovese, 148
Santa Barbara (California)
Pinot Noir, 115
Syrah, 125
Santa Maria Valley
(California), Syrah, 125
Santa Ynez Valley
(California), Syrah, 125
Sassicaia (Tuscany), 97
Sauternes, 166
Sauvignon Blanc, 59
Australia, 66
California, 64
Casablanca, Chile, 65
food pairing, 66
Fumé Blanc, 65
Loire Valley, 60-62
New Zealand, 62-64
rival wines, 141
South Africa, 65
Scheurebe, 142
Selection de Grains
Nobles, 166
set Gaia (Australia), 97
Sherry, 171
Shiraz
Australia, 122-124
California, 126
costs, 123
Sierra Foothills (California), Zinfandel, 134
sipping wine (tasting tip),
12-13
Skouras Megas Oenos
(Greece), 97

Smaragd (Wachau Riesling), 75

smelling wines (tasting tip), 11

sniffing wines (tasting tip), 11

sommeliers
    roles, 32-38
    tipping, 42

Sonoma (California)
    Cabernet Sauvignon, 95
    Zinfandel, 132

Sonoma Coast (California), Pinot Noir, 115

South Africa, Sauvignon Blanc, 65

Southern Rhône appellations (France), Syrah, 121-122

Spain, sparkling wines, 158-159

sparkling wines
    Blanc des Blancs, 155
    Blanc des Noirs, 155
    California, 160
    Champagne, 156-158
    costs, 158
    forcing bubbles, 151-154
    Italy, 159
    New Mexico, 160
    Rosé, 155
    Spain, 158-159
    sweet wines, 161-163
    sweetness, 155-156
    vintage versus nonvintage, 154-155

Spätburgunder, 116

Spätlese (Prädikat level), 70

spitting wine (tasting tip), 13

St-Aubin appellation, 52

St-Éstephe appellation (Bordeaux, France), Cabernet Sauvignon, 91

St-Joseph appellation (Rhône Valley), Syrah, 120

St-Julien appellation (Bordeaux, France), Cabernet Sauvignon, 92

St-Veran appellation, 52

Standing Stone (New York State Riesling), 76

Steinfeder (Wachau Riesling), 75

Stellenbosch (South Africa), Sauvignon Blanc, 65

straight corkscrews, 5

sulfite statements (wine labels), 30

Sutter Home Zinfandel, 133

swallowing wine (tasting tip), 13

sweet wines
    botrytized wines, 165-166
    Chenin Blanc, 164
    fortified, 168-171
    Gewürztraminer, 165
    Riesling, 163-164
    Sherry, 171
    sparkling wines, 161-163
    Tokaji, 166-167
    vin de paille, 167
    Vinsanto, 167
    Viognier, 165

sweetness
    Prädikat levels, 69-70
    sparkling wines, 155-156

swirling wines (tasting tip), 11

Switzerland, Merlot, 105

Syrah
    Australia, 122-124
    California, 124-126
    costs, 121, 127
    Rhône Valley, France,
      119-122
    rival wines, 148-149
    styles, 119
    versus Petite Sirah,
      126-127
    Washington State, 127

T

tank method, forcing bub-
  bles in sparkling wines, 152
Tannat, 145
tannic wines, 99
Tasmania region (Australia),
  Pinot Noir, 117
tasting tips, 9
    affects of climate on
      taste, 146
    restaurants, 36
    sipping, 12-13
    sniffing, 11
    spit or swallow, 13
    swirling, 11
    taking notes, 13, 16
Tawny Port, 171
Tempranillo, 148
terroir, Chardonnay, 49-50
tipping sommeliers, 42
Tocai Friulano, 142
Tokaji, 166-167
Tokay Pinot Gris, 80
Torronte, 141
Touriga Nacional, 146
tracing wine bottles, 29

traditional method, forcing
  bubbles in sparkling wines,
  152-154
Trebbiano, 144
Trentino-Alto Adige region
  (Italy), Pinot Grigio, 82-83
trocken (dry), 70
Trockenbeerenauslese, 166
Trockenbeerenauslese
  (Prädikat level), 70
Twin Islands Pinot Noir, 118

U–V

United States wines
    California. *See* California
    New York State, 76, 117
    Oregon, 84-85, 114
    Washington State, 104,
      127

Vacquerays appellation
  (Rhône Valley), Syrah, 122
varietals (grapes), 23
VDN (vin doux naturel),
  168-169
Vega Sicilia Único (Spain),
  97
Veneto (Italy), Pinot Grigio,
  81
Verdicchio, 144
Vermentino, 140
Victoria region (Australia)
    Pinot Noir, 117
    Shiraz, 123
vin de paille, 167
vin doux naturel. *See* VDN
Vinsanto, 167

vintage
    sparkling wines, 154-155
    wine labels, 24-26
Viognier, 140, 165

W

Wachau vineyards
    (Austria), Riesling, 74-76
Wairarapa region (New
    Zealand), Pinot Noir, 116
waiter's friend corkscrews,
    5-6
Walla Walla (Washington
    State), Merlot, 104
warm-climate Chardonnay,
    48
Washington State
    Merlot, 104
    Syrah, 127
white wines
    bargain wines, 139
    Chardonnay, 46-57
    Pinot Gris, 143-144
    Riesling, 67-76, 142
    Sauvignon Blanc, 141
    Zinfandel, 129-131
wine labels
    back labels, 29
    checking in restaurants,
        34
    grape variety, 22
    quality classifications,
        26-28
    sulfite statements, 30
    vintage, 24-26
    where wine is from,
        18-23
    winery names, 24

wine lists. *See* lists (wine)
wineries
    Château Mouton-
        Rothschild, 92
    location of name on
        wine bottle, 24
winged double-lever pulls
    corkscrew, 6

X-Y-Z

Yakima Valley (Washington
    State), Merlot, 104

Zind-Humbrecht vineyard
    (Alsace, France), Riesling,
    73
Zinfandel
    old vine wines, 132-133
    origins, 129-131
    pink wines, 129-131
    Primitivo, 135
    red wines, 131-134
    rival wines, 149
    White Zinfandel,
        129-131
    winegrowing regions,
        131-135
Zweigelt, 147